D1547991

PUBLISHING & PRINTING
AT HOME

PUBLISHING &
PRINTING AT HOME

ROY LEWIS &
JOHN B. EASSON

photographs by
ROGER BENNETT

DAVID & CHARLES
Newton Abbot   London   North Pomfret (Vt)

Photoset in 10/12pt Century Schoolbook on
Linotype-Paul CRTronic
Printed offset litho on Royal Sabre coated cartridge
115gsm

British Library Cataloguing in Publication Data

Lewis, Roy, 1913–
    Publishing & printing at home.
    1. Printing, Practical   2. Publishers and
    publishing
    I. Title   II. Easson, John B.
    070.5   Z244

    ISBN 0 7153 8510 0

Typeset by ABM Typographics Limited, Hull
and printed in Great Britain
by Billings & Sons Ltd, Worcester
for David & Charles (Publishers) Limited
Brunel House   Newton Abbot   Devon

Published in the United States of America
by David & Charles Inc
North Pomfret   Vermont 05053   USA

CONTENTS

1
PUBLISHING FOR PLEASURE

The spare-time publisher

This book is about the craft of publishing books, booklets and periodicals in small editions from one's own backroom or backyard. It is a leisure pursuit or an occupation for retirement that is as suited to home operations as weaving, pottery, cabinet-making, metalwork or photography and comparable creative pastimes.

It can be done on a very small scale, or it can be as absorbing of time and love as gardening. It can be, or become, a sideline business, and make or lose money in the manner of other sideline businesses. Its products can make a reputation for its practitioner, and it should lead to new experiences and friendships. It deals in self-expression and is itself a form of self-expression.

As in professional publishing, women can and do excel in it. Irrespective of gender, it is something one can begin at twelve or at sixty — and continue beyond the eighties.

It is not in the least beyond the scope of people with disabilities; those who wish to do some of the production at home (see Chapter 5) can select the processes which can be adapted to their abilities.

Like other crafts or small businesses conducted in one's leisure time, publishing requires some outlay of money. How much or how little depends on the nature and scale of one's operations and ambition. It can be minimal: several of the most prestigious examples of small publishing began with no capital beyond a set of tools, scrap wood, skill and a few shillings (when shillings bought something) spent here and there. Today a small press and publishing unit can certainly be set up for a fraction of the outlay some people lavish on hi-fi equipment.

The space that it takes up in one's home depends on whether the publisher puts all the printing and binding operations out to commercial printers, in which case a desk and a storage area pretty well suffice; or whether one decides to do some or all of the production and printing at home, which will require a room, cellar, attic or garden shed to be set aside for the work. We have seen it done in a caravan. We know a young Scottish lady who operates a publishing, printing *and hand-paper-making* complex in her bed-sit!

There are many choices, beguiling possibilities, all sorts of byways down which one can be led. For publishing is relevant to so many other crafts, arts and activities. To authorship, obviously. But also to many forms of visual art (and even music), photography, bookbinding and bibliophilia in its protean forms.

We hope to look at all these, and from current practice in 'small', 'independent', 'little', or 'home' publishing we shall offer suggestive examples of the work that is being done.

We hope to show how the money available can be spent to go furthest at every option the small publisher faces. His choices will be guided not only by his personal tastes, but also by the time and cash at his disposal, because in this — as in other one-man or one-woman crafts that involve manufacture — time and money are substitutes for each other.

Therefore throughout this book we shall try to provide estimates of the money *and* time expended in every operation that the spare-time publisher can undertake for himself or contract out although admittedly such estimates must be elastic. We shall probably expose some personal bias towards operating on a shoe-string, or at least on a penny-wise budget, with a proportionate reliance on personal labour and one's own time. People of means can do what they like, of course; the prices of new equipment will indicate how much they can spend when money is not restricted.

Most people taking up a hobby have to think carefully about costs. The loss of a shoe-string project, whether from a change of circumstance, failure of energy, of interest, or of market, is no very great disaster; one can cut one's losses and seek a more congenial pastime.

There is another reason for doing things economically. One learns much more, and when money is later spent for improved quality or larger output, it is spent more knowledgeably.

We live in the age of DIY. It was quite usual for the Victorian self-publisher or private press innovator, not only to buy his equipment for printing but to hire one or more journeymen printers to do the work. One such worthy, Sir Thomas Phillips, who had £8,000 a year (and income tax at 2p in the £) paid his printer 30s (£1.50) a week in 1850, which, however, was more than he paid his cook. The age of cheap labour is long over. This point, the cost of buying someone else's time (eg in the form of the cornershop instant printer), is pivotal to the cost comparisons we shall discuss.

For every creative temperament and talent there is an appropriate craft or spare-time interest. Not everyone has an urge to be a publisher or editor. On the other hand, a number of people who would enjoy publishing, and have clear ideas of what they would publish, have little conception of what the process involves. They are daunted by a feeling

Brian Louis Pearce

The Vision of
Piers Librarian

Woodruff
1981

Fig 1 Example of a title page to a booklet of 32 pages, the first publication from a home publisher equipped with a hand press and hand-set type operated by the poet's wife with no previous experience of print

that it is too expert, complex and costly an undertaking to consider. That is a better starting-point than the belief that with the aid of the instant printer it will be easy, cheap and not at all time-consuming.

The facts are that publishing on a modest budget is perfectly possible and can be readily learnt (both authors are largely self-taught). What is no less pertinent, and may be stressed at the outset, is that it is equally possible, and should be the aim, to publish and print books and booklets — 'slim volumes' — which in appearance measure up closely to the current standards of the professionally manufactured book. Some private presses set themselves to out-do the professional standard, emphasising the better appearance of a book printed by letterpress on hand-made paper, and they command correspondingly high prices for their books, as traditionally they always have.

Scores of small presses, not quite so dedicated, successfully publish good-looking and charmingly designed books from their owners' homes. Some have long lives, others short. Some issue a dozen titles, others a hundred or more. Many distinguished and memorable books have been given to the world by this route — and many have done it on the proverbial shoe-string.

Plate 1 Slim volumes: a selection of books from the independent and private presses indicating variety of subjects and bookmanship in presentation

Publishing and self-publishing

We must here try to make clear the relationship between publishing and self-publishing. This book is not a guide to certain forms of self-publishing: such manuals are already available. Authors whose books, fiction or non-fiction, which have been rejected by commercial publishers (often called 'trade houses' or the 'Trade') sometimes decide to bring them out themselves, a procedure they all too often suppose amounts to little more than finding a cheap printer and saying 'Here's the typescript, let there be a book, two thousand copies should do for the first edition.'

The outcome is usually a humiliation. Even if neither author nor printer can see it, the book looks amateurish, breaches the conventions of publishing and book layout, and commits other solecisms. No bookshop will take it, no reviewer glance at it. The author has lost his stake. Even if he pays only for a small edition for private circulation the result tends to be unimpressive and the cost out of all proportion.

Other authors, realising that printing and binding a book are only the first stages of a longish process, are seduced by certain 'vanity presses' who undertake not only the production but the publishing in the fuller sense of the term, for a sizable fee. A passable book emerges but still there are neither reviews nor sales. Authors contemplating such a recourse should be told — 'don't'.

There are exceptions to every rule, just as there are no hard-and-fast distinctions between the ways of bringing out the vast variety of books successfully. The odds against a self-published book gaining a readership of over a hundred are rather long. The self-publisher is generally really thinking of a 'small edition' as we define it, rather than a commercially published book. Henry Adams, the American historian, had his famous autobiography, *The Education of Henry Adams,* printed in an edition of a hundred copies for private distribution; it subsequently became a classic.

Authors as diverse and well-known as Gertrude Stein, John Galsworthy, Edmund Blunden, D. H. Lawrence, Rudyard Kipling and Edgar Allan Poe had, for various reasons, examples of their work privately printed and circulated. A leading example is *The Rubáiyát of Omar Khayyám:* when its author-translator could not get it accepted in the ordinary way he had it printed at his own expense, but without immediate result. It became a best-seller when D. G. Rossetti discovered it in Quaritch's remainder penny box. In another genre, Beatrix Potter paid £26 to have the first Peter Rabbit story printed, and thereafter became a world-renowned author.

Authors have not infrequently paid professional publishers to bring

11

out books with no evident viability under their commercial imprint. Robert Browning's father brought out the poet's first book in that way, and not one copy of *Paracelsus* was sold. The Brontë sisters had better luck — two copies of their jointly published and financed poems were sold. However, when Samuel Butler paid a publisher to bring out *Erewhon* anonymously it enjoyed runaway sales — until the literary world discovered that it was written by the obscure son of a bishop and not by Bulwer Lytton or Benjamin Disraeli. P. H. Gosse, however, made money by so operating and so, in different circumstances, did G. B. Shaw.

Some publishers continue this tradition occasionally, but generally a publisher will only put his imprint on a book on which he is prepared to risk his own money.

The private-press tradition

Avoiding the 'vanity press' trap, authors have set up their own presses or imprints to publish their work — perhaps alongside the work of like-minded writers. One reason may be that the presswork is part of the art form.

The exemplar is of course William Blake, who printed and published his own prophetic poetry and 'graphics' (to use the modern term for all illustration or visual counterpoint) in a way no printer of his day could have done, though it has been done in our time, because he kept the process a secret on the orders of the Angel who revealed it to him. The world was not impressed. Today he is a source of inspiration for many author-artist-poet-printers. Among his disciples was Ralph Chubb, whose work is pertinent to our theme: first because it was done on a shoe-string — his brother built him a press when he was unemployed; secondly he evolved a combination of several graphic processes; thirdly the editions were small (and commanded high prices). A modern artist in this tradition is Morris Cox, who adapts his presses to the requirements of his books.

A more usual motive is not the need to develop a graphic medium, but the conviction that one's work, ahead of its time, has a small if discriminating readership to which it must be addressed. An example is that of Leonard and Virginia Woolf who wanted, in 1917, to bring out their own work printed in their own way, and who, duly rejected by the trade schools, happened to pass the Excelsior Printing Supply Co, by accident, and were delighted to discover that one could buy a small printing machine, type and accessories along with an instruction book of sixteen pages. Self-taught, and for £38, they established the Hogarth Press in Richmond, an imprint that became so prestigious and so far out-

Exploring Surrey

THE MOLE VALLEY

Don Goodacre

with drawings by the author

© D. C. Goodacre. Published at 82 Queen Mary Avenue, Morden, Surrey SM4 4JR and printed by Roebuck Press, Kingston Road, Merton, Surrey.

Fig 2 Title page to one of a series of personal guides written, published and illustrated by Don Goodacre, using IBM Executive unjustified setting but line illustrations

grew the 'Model hand press' they had on their kitchen table, that it became a commercial publishing house — but not before that handpress had printed the first selection of T. S. Eliot's poems and a short story by Katherine Mansfield that took the critics by storm.

Similarly, the Seizin Press was set up by Laura Riding mainly to print Robert Graves's work, while Anaïs Nin printed her first novels and poems before a commercial publisher would have them: her response to the joys and chores of printing are charmingly written.

Other such presses have been set up to publish not its proprietor's work, but that of his friends — usually the *avant garde* work of a group. A distinguished case was the Hours Press of Nancy Cunard, who, like the Woolfs, taught herself letterpress printing and brought out books (in France) by a galaxy of talent then little recognised — Samuel Beckett, Louis Aragon, Ezra Pound, Richard Aldington and others.

We have thus proved, we hope, that the lineage of private and lay publishing is impeccable, and that snobs who think it infra dig are merely ill-informed. There is nothing cranky about it and it gives the lie to the adage that 'everything worth printing finds a publisher'. Unquestionably, it has mainly been concerned with the unusual, unconventional and unpopular at the time of publication and this has implied small editions.

Where, in the past, any part of the printing was done at home the edition had to be limited to hundreds. Hand printing and a small market — even such a market as 'Bloomsbury' — matched well, technically and economically. They still do. When in the past large volumes were called for, publishing *at* home became publishing *from* home: the commercial printer was called in — as happened to the Hogarth Press. Today, small printer-publishers find that a mix of home-produced and bought-out printing suits their varied needs. This book, therefore, will consider the best ways to get books, or sections of books, printed out (Chapter 4) as well as at home (Chapters 6–8).

The new printing

Publishing non-professionally in the past necessitated a grasp of the technique and craft of letterpress printing ('hot-metal setting', though this really refers only to composition by Lino- and Monotype: hand-setting is with cold metal). As indicated above, it should be clear that this is no mystery: all sorts of men and women have without formal apprenticeships mastered it. In essence it is a straightforward craft, and the equipment, new and especially second-hand, is easy to acquire. Yet an air of the arcane clings to it for many people; its jargon seems impenetrable, and even the textbooks that were issued to encourage the craft for schools and other institutions, looked difficult to those who wanted to bring out books and magazines. The alternative — cutting stencils with a typewriter to be used in the simpler forms of duplicator or mimeograph — was only suitable for ephemeral work, such as magazines, circulars, and examination papers!

This situation has been transformed by the 'printing revolution' in the last twenty years. Hot-metal setting by Linotype or Monotype has been almost superseded by the combination of offset-photolithography for the printing and photocomposition of texts (now alluded to as 'cold setting'). The advent of 'small offset' — small lithographic printing machines (see Chapter 7) has also given an incentive to the development of elaborate typewriter-composers, many incorporating electronic controls, which are also much used for setting book and magazine texts; these are now often described as 'strike-on' composers to distinguish them both from hot-metal composition and photocomposition: all machines which strike a character through a ribbon to transfer its image to paper may be grouped as strike-on systems.

Everybody knows what this has meant — the 'instant printer' who can take a poster, circular or typewritten leaflet and print it by offset-litho in exactly the form in which the customer presents it, in as many copies as he wants. What the customer hands in, good or bad in design or finish, is exactly what he gets back, multiplied to his order.

A leaflet contains some of the elements of a book. It is fairly easy even for an amateur to take a small printed book which is out-of-copyright but of fresh interest to an offset-litho firm and have it reproduced exactly; we know of an entrepreneur ignorant of publishing who did just that with an old but entertaining guide to the Thames and sold it in riverside pubs.

Another form of reproducing existing or old texts without resetting is to use the photocopier; the new generation of these, capable of printing on ordinary paper with increased speed, threatens to compete strongly with offset-lithography (see p. 129).

Methods of exploiting these processes, combined with the continued use of letterpress, make up the latter half of this book. Letterpress printing in the home is far from obsolete. Wise technologists say that the one certainty of introducing a new technology is the survival of the old technology. The bicycle survives as the best form of transport for many purposes — even in war.

The revolution which has transformed commercial printing and publishing has thus made very small publishing easier. This may seem a paradox. For the advantages of computerised typesetting and lithographic printing have enhanced the cost savings on long runs. This follows from the basic truth about printing economics: most of the cost is incurred before a single copy is delivered — the cost of composition, layout, imposition, plate-making, and preparing the machines to print. After the first copy the remaining extra costs are mostly the paper (which admittedly is getting more expensive) plus the running cost of the machine. The fall in the unit cost of a piece of printing, especially a book, proceeds faster by the new methods. Hot-metal composition and machining on a flatbed machine made a 1,000 to 5,000 run quite economical; now, the huge capital cost of modern machines makes printers hungry for long runs of books and they set the incentives in their estimates accordingly.

Nor is this the only factor that encourages large editions ('mass market books') and discourages small editions. Costs in other publishing operations have soared in recent years: administrative overheads, the costs of marketing and publicity, of warehousing and stock control. Books, in short, would be dirt cheap if only fifty titles were published each year in tens of millions of copies. In reality books remain small individual items, most of them produced in batches of a thousand or two. The publisher has to price accordingly and the public grumbles.

The small edition

We may have oversimplified the impact of the new processes on the publisher. Even so it has an important outcome. Very small editions of books, like small batches of many other desirable things, tend to get too expensive for the market, and so do not get produced at all. In the 1930s, with the old printing methods, a publisher could break even on a novel in a hardback edition of 600 or so priced at 7s 6d net. Now, sales of 3,000 to 5,000 are the 'breakeven point' for such an item, priced at £6.95. In vain publishers claim that £6.95 is relatively no dearer than 7s 6d. But the public sees it as such — and the actual market for that sort of novel may still be only 600 to 1,000 copies. The publisher therefore hunts for the sort of novels that easily sell 5,000 — which excludes many good novels (or so authors say).

Any small edition nowadays tends to lose money on its production cost unless the price can be set very high — £25 upwards — which is possible for some highly specialised books. Because all costs are up, the publisher needs to be sure his edition will sell out; his warehouse costs preclude

---

(*opposite*)
Plate 2 Four cover designs using different illustration techniques: (*top left*) *Fishing in the Sky* by Michael Longley, Poet & Printer Press, litho; (*top right*) *An Illustrated Guide to Space* by Neil Armstrong and others, published by Illustrated Guide Executive, litho; (*bottom left*) *Sez M'Mam* by Barry Heath, Your Own Stuff Press, litho; (*bottom right*) *Chill Air* by Spike Milligan, New Broom Press, letterpress

ishing in the sky
ove poems   Michael Longley

an
Illustrated
Guide

You need not begin with big or mysterious things.

TO

SPACE

2

M'MAM
SEZ BARRY HEATH

CHILL AIR

SPIKE MILLIGAN

Drawings by
RIGBY GRAHAM

NEW BROOM PRESS

him from keeping it in stock if it sells slowly, as some superb books always do. The book remainder shops testify to the need for rapid turnover (and so hit the ordinary bookseller a glancing blow).

So quite large gaps have opened which, with the help of both the old and new technologies, the small publisher, including the small home publisher, can usefully fill — some at a modest profit. The obvious field is poetry. But there are many others. An edition that is expensive waste paper in 5,000 copies may be an asset to culture in an edition of 350, and a sad loss if it remains in typescript.

In some walks of life, of course, a degree of small publishing goes with the job. The parish priest has his magazine; he may now recognise in its attraction a pastoral influence not less than that of his weekly sermon. Politicians have their constituency or ward news-letter, important when the voters were never so scandalously lax in party loyalty. The business which once could not afford a house organ now runs one off the office copier as an aid to worker-management understanding. And so on.

The bigness of bigness has created its own reaction. Economies of scale dictate mass-produced standards and choices: human cussedness responds by becoming more local and tribal and particular. There arises a demand for specialities, including hand-made books and alternative philosophies. The customer's realisation that one of the big firms has not churned out the book may sell it and its message. As choice is curtailed in one area, demand for 'something different' flares up in another.

Also, bigness breeds a sense that one is being kept out; that only a pushful or well-connected élite of talent can get itself published. It is important that all talent should test itself in print, if only once. We shall consider the marketing of small editions in Chapter 3.

How small is small? This is a question that must be asked at every stage in this book, because method, message and market interact all the time. For certain markets, using the appropriate equipment, a successful small edition may be 40 copies. If 2,000 can be sold, then the project calls for a commercial printer and will repay the cost, although the publisher will then run into all the cost restrictions that frustrate the large publisher. Our concern, in Chapter 5, is to review the choice of methods that suit the market and message, and that fit the market in the cheapest and most practicable way.

If that choice is to cut costs by undertaking part or all of the production processes at home, the ensuing chapters will show how it can be done. Chapter 8 extends these options into small periodical production.

Our emphasis is on creative enjoyment, not on making a second income. If money is the object, jobbing printing at home has long provided pocket or pin money for those who like printing so long as it makes money for them.

Books are different and call for a different approach, and for less elaborate equipment and procedures. Our suggestions for the use of minimal equipment and simplified procedures will undoubtedly upset some experts and purists. So be it. Such methods will produce books of merit if powered by imagination and skill.

But they *will* call for some hard work — nothing can be achieved without effort. Artists and craftsmen know this, as authors know it, even if educational theory eschews it. It is true of any hobby, from gardening to amateur opera. We hope to show how the chores can be cut to a minimum by careful pre-planning. But Shakespeare sums it up:

There be some sports are painful, which their labour
Delight in them sets off . . .

The proof of this is that there are in Britain over 130 small publishers who elect to print by letterpress rather than 'small offset', setting their texts by hand, and issuing two to four books a year: in the United States over 400 choose to do it Caxton's way, and there are many others in Europe and Australasia.

Small offset is, of course, the choice of very many more; the figure runs into thousands, if occasional publishing (a book every two or three years), is included. There are said to be 6,000 small publishers who make a living out of it. It has been proposed that those who do not make a living out of it, or by it, but publish for fun or for conscience, and yet more or less make ends meet, should be called 'the independent publishers'. But there are no sharp dividing lines. All one can say is that the more a spare-time publisher budgets for profits, rather than merely to avoid overheavy losses, the nearer to 'professional status' he moves. In choosing our illustrations we try to indicate the variety that there is, and the answers that each offers to challenges, rather than to demonstrate aesthetic criteria. Only an indication is possible, so great is the variety in style and status of home publishers.

19

2
THE SMALL EDITION

The economics of publishing on a shoe-string

The small edition, published from home, is inevitably limited in size, number of pages, and textual content. Of course a publisher, working from his study, can commission every process in book manufacture from editing the typescript to storage of the finished copies, and thereby issue substantial novels or lexicons under his own imprint. He may need a part-time secretary, but that is all.

Such a publisher, however, competes with the big and middle-sized publishing houses, making only moderate savings on overheads, since all his subcontractors — editors, designers, printers, binders, warehousemen, representatives and accountants — must pass on *their* overheads in their bills to him. He will save only his own salary, his personal overheads and maybe a sum consisting of a seventh of his house expenses and car, as tax-deductible costs. Such publishing is possible; especially if the publisher knows or can attract first-rate authors whose names sell their books. But he will need a lot of working capital and a trusting bank manager.

To make a *living* as a small publisher working from home (usually a man and wife team) requires an output of about twelve steady-selling titles a year, in specialities whose market the publisher knows intimately. He may then be able to afford a staff of one, and contract out all his printing, distribution and storage. This is the basis of the success of the 6,000 or so small commercial publishers mentioned above, some of whom are members of their own special association, the Independent Publishers' Guild. In our terms they are fully professional, and this book is not addressed to them; but into their ranks some home publishers, or 'little presses', with commercial flair, not infrequently graduate.

Publishing used to be described as a 'cottage industry' by its practitioners for this reason. The trends to hugeness, conglomeration and mass-production are pronounced, yet it remains a cottage industry. The cottages are of every size and shape: here we are concerned with the smallest, whether they are run to break even, or to make a small supplementary income or, as is nobly true of most, are run at a 'loss'. But whatever their criterion of success, they succeed because their owners can keep their overheads and direct costs far below that of the 'commercial cottages', and because they can identify a market for their books (or periodicals) which, however small, they alone can reach.

Output of the home publisher

This means that the home publisher produces relatively few titles and these fall mainly into the category of 'slim volumes'. We have admired a few novels and biographies of 180 pages and more published entirely from the back room; but insofar as they were one-man products, that one man could hardly produce more than one book a year, or one every other year. Most home-produced books run from 16 to 48 pages; and our estimate is that to produce and market three of these a year will consume something like one-third of a man's working time. (Or add a third *to* his working time if he does a full-time job as well.) If he goes in for 48-page books he may only be able to produce two per year. If he limits himself to 8-page pamphlets (still called 'chapbooks' in the USA) he may issue six or more a year. The reason is simple. For a publisher who keeps his costs low by undertaking some or all of the production himself — and in a way that yields him creative scope and a craftsman's satisfactions — there is a limit to the total number of *pages* he can print, whatever way he divides these up into thicker or thinner books.

Let us try to quantify the foregoing from our own and others' experience, taking the example of a simple letterpress plant. It is important because the equipment that a home publisher-printer elects to buy should be tailored to the work he means to turn out (Chapter 4). Even the smallest spare-time publisher has to spend a good proportion of his hobby time on work other than production.

A 16-page pamphlet of poetry can be originated in metal type by an experienced man or woman (or man-and-wife team) and printed off in 40–50 hours of work (say, two weekends). This includes setting the title page, cover, colophon, etc, imposing the type in chases (this procedure is explained in Chapter 9), pulling proofs, making corrections, and printing the run of, say, 250 copies. Assuming two pages are printed at a time, this is 8 runs, plus one for the cover. (Small presses generally print two pages at a time, so the small printer thinks in 'fours' — see Chapter 9.)

So two, perhaps three, weekends' work has produced a simple book complete in sheets for the final or 'finishing' stages of book manufacture. Allow another ten to fifteen hours for folding, assembling the sheets, and sewing them to covers (or sewing the sheets together and then gluing them to the covers), and trimming them with a card cutter or guillotine. Depending on the text, some 60 hours will have been spent; perhaps rather more.

A farm worker was sitting at the road side. One of the soles of his boots was coming off and he was trying to pull it off completely. He was cursing and swearing and pulling and tugging at his sole trying to free it from his boot.

When a minister on a bicycle coming along the road overheard him cursing and swearing, he stopped and said to him, "Where, my man, do you think your soul will go using language like that?". The farm worker replied, "If I can get it off my boot it's going over the bloody dyke!"

* * *

There was a farmer in Ayrshire with a small 60-acre dairy farm; the land was wet and very bad to drain because of rocks and bog. The farm had been bought in the thirties by the family and the present farmer didn't like it or the area very much; he only kept about twenty dairy cows on the farm as it wouldn't carry any more.

He had also been left quite a bit of money by an aunt, so he wasn't really very hard up. He was always looking in the press for a bigger and better farm and keeping his ears open when he was among farmers at cattle markets.

One day when he was reading a farming paper he came across a fairly large farm for sale outside Glasgow, so he made a few 'phone calls, asked when viewing was and how and when the farm was going to be sold. After considering all the facts he was very interested.

He thought he would go and look it over - first he went to see one of his neighbours; an old established farmer who had a good knowledge of land and was very well respected in the neighbourhood. The old farmer had never travelled very far in his lifetime; he was a farmer through and through, all he ever thought about and could talk about was farming.

Both farmers travelled to Glasgow by train, the old farmer had never been so far from home before. As they stepped off the train at St. Enoch railway station in Glasgow the old farmer stood and looked around, then turned to his neighbour and said, "By, this station would make a grand hay barn!" The farmer bought the farm privately and he is still there.

* * *

"If I can get it off my boot it's going over the bloody dyke!"

COAL MERCHANTS:

The distinction between the professional and the working shopkeeper is somewhat arbitrary and some shopkeepers possessed features of both these types. Mr. Grinyer's father, for example, though the employer of five men in a flourishing coal business, undertook some of the same tasks as his employees, and did not adopt the middle-class habits of other more typical professional shopkeepers. Mr. Grinyer's mother and brother also took an active part in the business.

How did your father take over the business? "Well, he worked for a man named Sergeant, and he worked for him for years, and he was a coal merchant. After that my father took the business over."

Gloucester Place, looking towards St. Peter's Church

What else did you sell? "Coal, coke and wood. We picked it up from the station- weighed it up, up there. We never had no storage- only in the coal shed- so we had to go to the station frequently- practically all day long, with five horses and carts. My brothers all worked in the business- all five of them- but they left the business in their twenties. We all started at twelve years of age. They was up the station, I had to get things ready for when he came home- load up coke and wood for him to take on his rounds- go round hawking. All through the streets up Albion Hill- he sold from horse and cart. I used to go along to school- take the orders out with a borrow- ¼ cwt. bags- deliver them- then come home for dinner and go to school again. Come home from school and carry on."

What was the work like? "We all, and the men, used to do other deliveries in the afternoon, see- they'd do furniture moving on the vans. We also did brick carting, sand carting. In the mornings they was all out hawking. Used to start 4:00 a.m. at the station weighing up and loading up five horses and carts before 8:00. 8:15 bell would go at the works- home and have breakfast, then we went out. Father went out hawking just the same. Me and mother used to go round collecting money and mother helped with the books... it was a profitable business."

"Men had to look after the horses - had to come in of a morning and water them. Sometimes Dad used to go down about 6:00 and water them and feed them. Often there wasn't much work in the afternoon - they never knocked off - there was always something to do - painting the vans up, washing them down, cleaning the harness. They'd finish about 5:00 or 6:00. I left school at 14 and worked up to

But to production we must now add the time needed for publishing. First, before production begins, there is time consumed in dealing with the author (and finding him or her). Some perfect texts may arrive by post from well-established names; but not often. Few letters take less than half an hour to compose, type out and mail, with a carbon copy accessibly filed for reference.

After agreeing with the author (remuneration if any, proof correction procedure, review copies etc) the text has to be edited and marked up (Chapter 5) and the book designed. After production is complete, the author's, reviewers' and complimentary copies are sent out with appropriate slips; then copies with invoices for customers who have put in orders. This is the equivalent of another 30 hours (two or three weekends') work. By this stage, some 80–90 hours have been spent.

The next investment in time is in the marketing. This is harder to estimate, as the next chapter will show. If the imprint is well-known, the list of standing orders for titles long, the edition small, then the marketing effort may consist only in sending out the copies labelled and securely packed in an appropriate way. However, we estimate that each takes up to 20 minutes to do, so that if 120 copies are posted singly, another 30–40 hours is consumed (hopefully, booksellers will be taking orders in threes and sixes).

Even a publisher whose titles 'go' thus swiftly will have to do some publicity, issuing a 'flier' or other announcement. If his author sells copies usefully at poetry readings some time is consumed organising supplies; visits to bookshops take up more time. This time can be spread over several titles, but for each it is not inconsiderable.

Nor is this quite the end of the 'time budget'. There is always a lot of 'general administration' in any hobby. In publishing at home, there is paper to be ordered, maintenance jobs to be done on the equipment, and type has to be distributed back into cases.

If the publisher is doing well, his books will generate a lively correspondence; all sorts of enquiries, useful and useless, from would-be writers asking advice and poets supplicating publication; entertaining and having literary fun generally. Aggregated, such 'time overheads' may easily add another ten hours' work to each title. To miss out on this is to miss out on a lot of fun.

All in all, the time taken to publish the 16-page booklet has probably taken well over 100 hours' work. Three such books will probably take

(*opposite*) ⸺

Plate 3 Books about local history and regional culture from independent publishers: (*top*) double-spread from *Muck-spreading* by Hunter Adair, published by Sun Studio, Cumbria; (*bottom*) double-spread from *Shops Book* by Neil Griffiths, published by Queenspark Books, Brighton

300 hours depending on the texts involved. At eight hours per day this represents about 40 working days, though spreading it over 4- or 5-hour days would be usual for a hobby. Assuming 280 full working days a year, this means 15–20 per cent extra 'working' time, if it can be so called. It represents nearly half the normal leisure time available after full-time work, taking everything into consideration. A retired or unemployed or partially employed person can look at it another way: such a publishing activity would take up 50 to 60 days of his year, though he can spread it more thinly over many more if he wishes.

A private-press owner, with some considerable experience, put it to us this way: he spent 20 hours setting a 2,500-word text by hand; 20 hours machining it in a 24-page format, and 10 hours on finishing (all stages in binding). If the text had been merely typed out, pasted up, and printed by an instant printer, but bound at home, clearly the production time might have been only 15 to 20 hours — for a much inferior-looking book. But that still leaves, on our reckoning, 50 hours for the publishing operations.

The importance, however, of labour-saving methods of production is obvious from the foregoing. It becomes more pressing when the publisher wishes to issue longer texts than sixteen pages of lyric poetry. When the option of typewriting and offset-litho was unavailable, long prose composition was beyond the scope of most home publisher-printers. This is no longer so, and much widens the scope of the home publisher (except those who insist on hand-set type as the mark of their work).

In all the above estimates, we have made no allowance for the extra time taken up when booklets are illustrated, calling for collaboration with artists, blockmakers, and so on (see Chapter 10).

If the binding goes beyond a simple paperback type of binding, the finishing stages, for which an allowance of ten hours was given above, will be much increased.

We hope that we have made a strong case for making both a time and a cost budget when planning to publish a book, or rather a series of books, from home. (Robinson Crusoe budgeted only in time-cost!) This will obviate causing disappointment to authors when books take longer than anticipated to appear. It will help to prevent the starting of ambitious books that never get finished at all. Above all it will help the spare-time and retirement publisher to work out just what his 'book-

---

(*opposite*) ——————————————————————————————
Plate 4 A sound preliminary exercise in book production by letterpress: broadsheets and poem cards from the New Broom Press, Leicester; Sycamore Press, Oxford; The Many Press, London; The Mandeville Press, Hitchin

THE MAN

I thought I saw Jesus
   on a tram
I said, "are you Jesus?"
   He said "yes I am."

© SPIKE MILLIGAN.

Drawing by Hans Erni.

Toni Savage of Leicester.
Foxville Rise Broadsheet Two, 1982.

THE CAT AND THE CANARY

John Willard

FEAR

Only the ignorant suffer through fear. Take a bird—a canary
in its cage—put it on a table—then let a cat jump up and
walk around the cage, glaring at the canary. What happens?
The canary, seeing its enemy so close to it, is frightened
almost to death. But if it had understanding, it would know
that the cat couldn't reach it while it had the protection of
the cage. Not knowing this, it suffers a thousand deaths—
through fear.

Drawing by Brian Allen

Printed by Toni Savage, Leicester for The Cat and the Canary,
produced and directed by Max Cotten, 14—23 April 1977.

Little Theatre Broadsheet Three, 1977.

Philip Larkin

Femmes Damnées

Sycamore Broadsheet 27

THREE ODES OF HORACE
TRANSLATED BY BILL SHEPHERD
Drawing by Martha Kapos

DRAGONCARDS
SERIES THREE

TWELVE POEMS BY -
Stewart Conn, Geoffrey Grigson, Madge
Hales, Jim Howell, Christopher Martin,
Katharine Middleton, Neil Powell, James
Reeves, C. H. Sisson, George Szirtes,
Anthony Thwaite and Donald Ward.

PRINTED ON COLOURED CARDS
AT THE MANDEVILLE PRESS, 2
TAYLOR'S HILL, HITCHIN, HERTS
Price 40p, Signed edition £1 - 50p

Poet on an Off-day

The excellent poet sat bright as a cake
- of lard - and nothing said.
And his vast excellence was lost
as all steered clear
of his tortoise-head.

Christopher Martin

capacity' is. He should have some idea how much overall time he can spare for any hobby or creative craft, and he can then allocate a proportion of the time for each book. This will facilitate the choice between paying a printer for all or part of the production, and doing it all himself.

Any commercial publisher who happens to glance through these pages may smile grimly and comment 'That'll larn 'em!'. Let him not do so. The amateur will put in far more work and overtime at nil pay than any of his employees. The home producer will toil at his case or tap his Varityper into the small hours when necessary and bully his wife to sew booklets until she contemplates divorce. How else have the ancient canals of Britain been restored? By volunteers whose efforts fill contractors and trade unionists with chagrin (their view being that either *they* should do the job for money, or, if there is no money, the job should *not* be done).

Besides, there is more leisure time now that there is less public money about. Many people have time for two or three time-consuming hobbies, as well as for holiday travel. There are occupations, like teaching, which have necessary time off for recreation — and home publishing is above all a recreation. There is earlier retirement. There is a medical call for therapeutic pursuits and craftwork to reduce 'stress' (or to provide more therapeutic stress). We do not claim that the pool of unemployed contains many potential publishers in our sense of the term — but it contains some, and, as we will show, financial limitations need not preclude them from plunging in. Some already have. In short — there is time. But it makes sense to use it wisely.

Authors and subjects

It can be assumed that spare-time publishing or the establishment of a private press implies that the founder knows who and what he or she wants to publish. If the interest is literary, he or she will know the writers, poets, artists and illustrators whose work requires the effort to bring it before the public. The *réclame* of Nancy Cunard's Hours Press in the 1930s derived from her connexions with the literary *avant garde* of her day — she began with the encouragement of a family friend, George Moore. The same is true of many home imprints today, such as Harry Chambers' Peterloo Poets, or Bernard Stone's Turret Books. It is typical of other imprints and presses.

It may come about differently. As a small imprint becomes established, authors will send in manuscripts. The appraisal and editing of these is an important job, and one that commercial publishers say is rewarding and suggestive, even when they accept barely one in fifty unsolicited typescripts. The home publisher, bringing out his books for pleasure, not profit, should be similarly discriminating and make his viewpoint plain. One should *never* do anything in this field that one does not enjoy. Hence the attraction of self-publishing to the exclusion of outside authors for some happy spirits. Choosing authors is at any level difficult; we have refused authors we now much regret — and this is a hindsight not unknown to the most famous publishers in the land. The smallest publisher will face, incidentally, the quirks of authors, their strange vanities and curious ingratitude for work done on their behalf, as much as the biggest publishers. It is usually the best-established and best-known authors who are most considerate. It is quite amusing for a scholar-publisher to find himself treated by an author as if he were a rather refractory tradesman; we all need to learn humility!

A home publisher who wants to specialise in a subject may have to seek authors. This will take time, the study of the journals and bibliographies that deal with that subject, and postage.

The case of the small periodical is discussed more fully in Chapter 8. It is usually created by a group, or sometimes *for* a group, that has a shared interest or purpose or credo. Their problem is not to fill the space and time available but the other way round. However, the editor-publisher, a distinctive sub-species of mankind who is generally driven by powerful and obscure inner urges, will have to spend a lot of time getting authors to write the articles they have promised, and to write them to deadlines, sub-editing them and cossetting them.

The time spent in getting and dealing with authors (and artists) is crucial to establishing an imprint: it builds the reputation of the publisher for producing genuinely worth-while books and booklets in his chosen field. Even if his niche is tiny, a publisher needs to get known in it. After all, he is in competition with every other publisher, from HMSO and the BBC downwards for readers and publicity. One or two booklets, published now and then, have to be resoundingly good to maintain an imprint — or the publisher himself has to enjoy notoriety, such as that he is a media celebrity, socialite, or an earl. Most imprints are established over time by consistency of purpose and presentation, whether they need recognition in a county or a continent. This is a hobby which, to yield its richest satisfactions, needs to be kept up for several years.

With all these factors worked out, the home publisher, skilfully cutting his production and administrative costs, has the small-edition market virtually to himself, if by the small edition we mean editions of books and booklets of some originality, of 50 to 500 copies. For only when the price of a book limited to 500 copies can be set at £50 to £150 net can a commercial publisher remuneratively enter this market. Of course there are specialised books, bibliographic or technical, which can be sold for £100 in editions of under 500, but these are indeed specialised.

27

The variety of the small edition

The range of the small edition is very wide, as the available reference books show. Contemporary poetry, as minority art, is the most obvious; the commercial publishers now produce relatively few titles, mostly subsidised, for (in the main) a small group of established poets (some of whom are publishers), and even they admit (privately) that it is hard work to sell 750 copies. There are exceptions, like Sir John Betjeman and Mary Wilson. Most commercial poetry publishing is school-book publishing. The established poets, in the big-time, tend to be patronising towards the army of poets who get no further than the little presses, though even the big men often patronise a small press if they like the company they keep.

In recent years, the little presses have claimed to put out 90 per cent of the poetry published in Britain. Sales of 250–350 are very good going for most of them. And our guess is that the difference between the sales of a poetry book published by a commercial imprint and one by a well-established little press is little more than 200 copies, due mainly to the big man's ability to coax more copies into reluctant bookshops.

The little presses have served poetry well; the poetry revival of the 1960s, as Edward Lucie-Smith has said, was both cause and effect of the spread of what he called 'the small imprints'. He noted that the better and more expensive the production the more conservative the choice of text has tended to be; much contemporary verse which has lasted first appeared in 'shoddy guise'. This need not continue to happen.

Poetry may have been the main thrust of small-edition publishing, but it is only necessary to look at the American *International Directory of Small Presses* to see that the range of other subjects is almost as wide as that of 'the Trade'. It lists over 15,000 titles in print (of which 20 per cent is poetry) and this leaves out the bulk of British production. It is impossible to guess the real total published in this way in the English language. It is said in 'the Trade' that there are 250,000 to 300,000 commercially published books in print, so the contribution of the various varieties of home publishers and printers is not negligible.

We can but quote a few examples to suggest the subjects that home publishers are interested in. There are, for instance, 700 fiction titles in print. On the other hand, under the language heading, there is nothing on the world's major tongues, but their exists a book on how to speak Cornish and phrasebooks on how to swear in Japanese. Specialist

(*opposite*)
Fig 3 Linocut illustration by Paul Piech for a title page giving greater impact than might be achieved by display type (*War Poems of Wilfred Owen*, Perdix Press)

PERDIX PRESS
SUTTON MANDEVILLE
SALISBURY, WILTSHIRE
1983

jargons, like that used in Citizens' Band (CB) radio or in sailing boats, find a lexicon; and there are manuals that clearly only justify very small editions such as knife-fighting, the all-seaweed cuisine, and on man-carrying kites.

The flexibility of offset-litho methods is shown by the way small publishers, just as much as large firms, exploit the coffee-table market for reproductions of old photographs and postcards; some people, who have collected these in the course of visits to the elderly, perhaps involved in social studies, have produced successful books in this way. An extension of this technique is shown in the imaginative use of photo-montage to convey a satirical or other message.

The influence of home computers is evidently not entirely anti-book: there have been published many small manuals of home-made computer programs and games.

In recent years there has been a boom in local history, archaeology, industrial archaeology and folklore societies: where there is enthusiasm, monographs are generated. The established scholarly journals cannot print all of even the most competent of these; the overflow has led to much self-publishing or group-publishing; and home publishers have found a useful place here. Many of the otherwise interesting studies put out by local field societies amount to little more than offset-litho or photocopier printed sheets of A4 paper typed by typewriter with a few drawings of maps or smudgy photographs, the whole stapled into paper covers down one side. The result is not a book and is wearisome to read: but the home publisher can make a real book of it, and some do, and increase the credit of all involved.

Associated with local history and topographical studies are the many parish-church brochures on their history and architecture. Often they say more than Pevsner can. Such booklets are a source of funds. Yet many are a poor advertisement for the vicar's knowledge of printing and bookselling. Others, however, reveal at once that the man of God has noted the brisk marketing of guides, slides and holy kitsch offered at the entrances of our great cathedrals and made almost impossible *not* to buy; and has done likewise on a smaller scale.

Hardly less fascinating is the history of many villages, apart from the church itself. Visitors would often pay to know more about the villages whose inns and pubs they patronise as well as the church. They cannot be expected to read it up in the official county history, but often the history has much of the material for a booklet that will sell for a pound or so in the gift-shop.

The municipalities of historic towns sponsor guides: these are frequently appalling as well as inaccurate, and the local printer turns out a wretched job on glossy paper. There is now a central organisation trying to latch on to this market which even offers 'scholarly research'; but the local scholars and social historians, and the long memories of the elderly, can produce far better material: real knowledge, racy writing, illustrations imaginatively culled from local archives and printed by a home publisher, can beat official productions hollow. For a tourist trap, of course, editions of several thousand are worth while, and we have seen local publishers rise to this challenge with the aid of offset-litho techniques. The 'short and simple' annals of our ancient villages do not call for elaborate printing; the home publisher can do it.

An expert with an important speciality will generally seek a fully commercial small publisher for his texts; but there are specialities which warrant only an article in a journal of interest to a few hundred or perhaps only a score of readers: if it is worth reprinting, the home publisher can usefully put it out. It is pleasant to see such small booklets selling alongside the mass products of big publishers.

Humour and gift books

There is apparently an endless demand for what we may call 'stocking fillers': inexpensive but original little items to be bought in gift-shops for odd occasions as well as the Christmas orgy. It is quite an industry, the stuff being churned out in every plastic shape by big firms with teams of designers gifted with scant taste. But this market contains within itself a market for small and charming books (as well as for the bookplates and greetings cards some distinguished presses print for discerning customers).

It is a market in which the home publisher can certainly compete if he has some flair for salesmanship. In humour, satire and invention he is — by definition almost — far superior to the funny-ideas men of the 'novelty' industry. A private press we know of, published, from an American computer print-out, a dictionary of 'Sod's Laws' (the humour of all of which turns on the discovery by *Punch* in 1883 that when a buttered bun falls on the carpet it always falls buttered-side down). After being wryly mentioned in the *British Medical Journal* (of all places) it sold like hot cakes until overtaken by a big-publisher's paperback on the subject.

This market is perhaps best exploited by the publisher with his own letterpress, rather than litho, equipment. A letterpress printing-machine can be adapted to cut out and crease all sorts of shapes in card or stiff paper. Ron King's Circle Press produces 'pop-up' books as part of its service to artists and exports them successfully.

To the letterpress-machine owner also goes the market in miniature books. These are books which do not exceed an 'official' height of

Popoffka

A plate of pies
with 4 propellers

A water-ballet
in the round.

De laude horti
In praise of the garden

Asmenius

Although they were both the
size they wanted they were
very miserable because of
having to leave their lovely
cave that day.

threefold

ELIZABETH II   NUMISMATA

NO
FREE WILL
IN TOMATOES
Peter Payack

GO
LD

THE CORN WAS
orient and immortal wheat, which
never should be reaped, nor was
ever sown. I thought it had stood
from everlasting to everlasting.
The dust and stones of the street
were as precious as gold; the gates
were at first the end of the world.
The green trees when I saw them
first through one of the gates
transported and ravished me, their
sweetness and unusual beauty made
my heart to leap, and almost
mad with ecstasy, they were such

Plate 6 Miniature books: a modern 'infant's library' of 30 books measuring 4¼in x 2½in by members of the Society of Private Printers; boxed as shown, it sold for about £75

3 inches, with the width in proportion. Their value increases as they are made smaller down to an inch high, and even a quarter of that. This category of 'toy book' has a history, and a collector's lore, going back to the seventeenth century; it made sense when a man wanted to take enough reading-matter to suffice a long trip on horseback. Special tiny type has even been cast for the purpose, but anyone with good eyesight and some 6-point type can play. To please the experts, however, the books today must be exquisite. Whole series are made, at high prices, marrying the skills of printer, bookbinder and cabinet-maker. Those with a penchant for miniaturisation are well advised to examine the comprehensive collections held by the British Library and the Bodleian Library as yardsticks of the quality called for.

(opposite)
Plate 5 Small formats and giftbooks: *Mailed Pinkle* by Finlay and Hincks from Verlaggerie Leaman (humour); *In Praise of the Garden* by Asmenius, from Demi-Griffin Press (giftbook); *A Tale of Two Witches* from Alembic Press (children); *Ten to One* by Steve Wheatley, from Caligula Books (humour); *Numismata* from Cuckoo Hill Press (typographic experimentation); *No Free Will in Tomatoes* by P. Payack, from Quark Press (epigrams); *Centuries of Meditation* by T. Traherne, from Old Stile Press (pensées)

Copyright and old texts

The texts of most limited editions are original and therefore copyright; so are the accompanying graphics, and so is the publisher's layout, which can only be reproduced by permission. Home printers are sometimes careless about inserting the copyright sign and formula on the verso of the title page, or elsewhere in the book. This is unwise if full international copyright protection is desired.

Accordingly care must be taken when reprinting old texts facsimile. There is a market for reprinting old texts where the design, illustration and typography are rated as important as, or even more important than, the message. Offset-litho techniques have increased the ease with which this can be done: Scolar Press has been the leader in this field.

We ourselves see little point, or much fun, in reprinting the classics, or bits of them, when one has the power to bring new work before the public, however limited that public may be. However, presses that cater mainly for the collector's and bibliophilia market (see p 49) do not agree; they argue that there is little point in lavishing craftsmanship and money on modern texts that nobody can assert will live as, for example, John Donne's poems have lived. This editorial policy plays safe, but attracts the reproach that it lives in the past, emulating William Morris and the post-Morris masters, who are hard to surpass. If some little-known masterpiece is unearthed by the home publisher it is obviously worth all the craftsmanship he can lavish on it. But it is important to observe the law of copyright in texts and know what is, and what is not, in the 'public domain' (ie out of copyright; see also p49).

The opportunities of the new printing technologies for artists and illustrators are great and we refer to these briefly in Chapter 10. The big publishers alone can afford fine-art colour reproduction. But this leaves scope for the ingenious up-and-coming artistic rebel, to whom offset-litho and silkscreen methods offer scope for experiment in small editions of the 'livre d'artist' in the French term.

No mention has been made of political pamphleteering, a noble tradition. Small editions and political lampooning or protest would seem a contradiction in terms in our mass democracy where political nostrums are sold in the media like canned beans. In fact, minority political argument is catered for by the 'community publishers', 'community printshops' and quite a sprinkling of 'alternative bookshops', which partly fall into our field insofar as they are partly non-commercial, or loss-making, in their operations; but they are rarely one-man shows. Like periodicals they are co-operative ventures, and often well-capitalised, using sophisticated equipment paid for out of public funds or charity. They are highly political and almost exclusively left-wing.

They interpenetrate the other advocates of the 'alternative society' which is not necessarily left-wing at all. These alternatives to mainstream behaviour require a great many small editions of books, pamphlets and periodicals to promote their prospectuses. The quality of production of these is often a poor advertisement for the utopias they promise. There are therefore subjects and authors in this field for the spare-time publisher; and the recent impact of mass unemployment on individuals will eventually produce good stuff. Also suited to the home publisher is the individual crusade — such as the defiant pamphleteering of the Melissa Press of Count Potocki of Montalk. We must hope, however, that the day will not come when the purpose of home (or cellar) publishing will be to print what Big Brother's censorship (right, left or alternating) prohibits.

3
SELLING THE SMALL EDITION

The market for books

Some of the books and even periodicals from little presses and home publishers are not marketed. They are given away to members of the societies that publish them or have them published. There are semi-captive readerships for some, even when a subscription is solicited, like house journals and some parish magazines. Not a few hand-made books are friendship offerings.

Such special situations apart, books and booklets should never be given away. Merely giving away a book will not establish how people rate its worth. The acid test is whether they will pay for it — if not in cash, at least in kind. The object of publishing is the marketing of a book, preferably not at a loss. It should be so even of an edition of 25 copies. No book has been tested until it has somehow been put up for sale.

On this subject all little presses, private presses and home publishers are agreed: their major problem is marketing and distribution. This need not surprise them. It is also the major problem and even obsession of almost every professional publisher. It has always been so, at least since printing began. But the electronic 'McLuhanist' age has brought a new worry: is the printed book itself obsolescent? Television, video-recorders, radio, computers, have all bitten into the market inasmuch as they have bitten into the public's reading-time.

The educational establishment retorts that more people are educated and need to read more than ever: they, the educationalists, claim to be increasing the reading public. Critics retort that modern education produces semi-illiterates who suppose books are classroom furniture to be discarded when one escapes into the real world.

This acrimonious dispute is over the heads of the publishing group which aims to sell editions of two to five hundred; still it is relevant, for even to sell a few hundred books is to compete for the public's eyes, ears and purse. The home publisher has his advantages. He is not in the market for mass-produced books, and is rarely aiming at the shelves of W. H. Smith (although there are exceptions here; see p 41). Outside the market for mass-produced and best-selling titles, there is no single 'market' for books in the sense that there are TV ratings. The book market is a congeries of markets. It can be likened to a street market with scores of little stalls all selling different objects. The small publisher's problem is to find his particular stall and get his offerings onto its counter. This image is concrete: the actual market is diffuse and scattered, even international, hard to find, and buying and selling (so to speak) in penny numbers.

The bookshops

Let us begin with the bookshop, which is almost (but not quite) the be-all and end-all of the commercial publisher producing what are called 'trade books' — that is ordinary books in commercial quantities. The broad view of home publishers, little presses and private presses is that it is impossible to get their books, however well produced, but with minor imprints inevitably, into bookshops. It is a hopeless task, they say; and a disagreeable one.

But why is it hopeless? In analysing the answer to that question, the home publisher and the way-out little press will alike learn much about the proper way to run their own operations. In fact it is *not* impossible to get small editions into *some* bookshops. It is hard work. It is work that must begin at the planning stage of the most unassuming publication. This is vital. The mutual relationship between bookseller and publisher must be understood because the feedback is so creative — mostly for the publisher. We have found that the minority author and/or publisher rarely takes the trouble to understand the great and growing problems of booksellers. He thinks they are not his worry. He is wrong.

He is doubly wrong if his attitude contains the slightest hint of hostility. The bookseller, not the publisher, is the hero of the embattled book trade. He is in the trenches. If anyone, glancing through this book, feels he would not like to take up publishing, but would like to fight for books as a cause, we would say: be a bookseller! It is a monstrous thing to say to any innocent, and this is not a manual of bookselling but we would concede that it is a finer thing to put one's time and money into bookselling than into publishing and we would be the first to cheer (and to stifle our fears for) any reader who elects to sell rather than make books. Indeed spare-time and home-based bookselling is as possible as spare-time publishing — but that is another story.

It is very hard indeed to make one's living as a bookseller. We include in the Bibliography some books about it that are worth reading. The bookseller, broadly, is in the business of selling thousands of quite disparate objects each of which has a small market of its own. His customers have, as already mentioned, some 250,000 separate items or titles which can be ordered. Most of these are in wholesale warehouses.

Only a very substantial bookshop can stock much more than 25,000 of these at any one time. Generally it will be less, because while the bookseller may have shelving for 25,000 books, he will keep several copies of the steady-selling items. Titles that he has not got he must order from the publishers.

Many bookshops, in despair, have now become little more than agents for the big paperback publishers, who bring them regular supplies of their books, load them into the shelves, and a month or two later the van comes round to fill the gaps, remove those that are still unsold and replace them with faster-selling titles. The bookseller is paid the mark-up (or trade discount) on titles sold, and his function as a book specialist is minimal. The plan is to computerise the whole operation and book covers now carry stock codes like other items of merchandise.

Such book merchandising and standardisation makes it possible for quite small or general stores to carry a shelf or a metal display stand of brand-name mass paperbacks and sell them as if they were toilet rolls or tights.

The reason is simple: there is money to be made on the mark-up of standard-coded packaged consumer items, but little on individual books. Publishers have little option but to try to treat their goods as standard merchandise, the faster the turnover the better. Inexorably they have been forced into a struggle to find best-sellers as such standard fast-selling lines. Many absurdities have resulted.

Selling serious books in singles at £5 to £15 each, as traditionally was done at the prices then ruling, and with knowledge of books and authors and availability, has become barely profitable. Customers are fewer, postage and overhead costs have soared, and really educated shop assistants are hard to find at salaries the bookseller can pay (in Germany they have degrees!). So the number of such true bookshops dwindles. Many large towns can only support one — some, in our more savage regions, none at all.

Yet it is to such bookshops that the home publisher must take his wares unless he comes up with a best-seller. He is a specialist producer and must market through a specialist seller. Two rules he therefore must abide by: he must offer rather better terms than his commercial rival who is represented by a skilled travelling salesman of books; secondly, in appearance his books must stand reasonable comparison with his professional competitor's offerings.

This may seem an impossible set of conditions — particularly for a man or woman who wants to *enjoy* book-making and publishing at leisure. It is not: that is the theme of this book.

Consider first the discount. The professional publisher offers from 17 to 35 per cent on the net price, depending on circumstances. It is simple to match that. But nowadays a 35 per cent discount on a £1.00 pamphlet represents a dead loss to a bookseller. One hardly improves the situation if one offers 40 per cent. Probably 50 per cent should be the proportion — the 50/50 split. Obviously the bookseller will be more amenable if he sees his way fairly easily to selling ten copies; further, he is liable to be more interested if the publisher can show him five or ten titles, rather than try to plug just one.

Here the upmarket private presses producing letterpress and hand-made paper books with really good (and perhaps mildly erotic) wood engravings in fine bindings at a price for the collectors' market of £10 to £100 have more to offer booksellers, provided the books can be sold at all. But many little presses, dedicated to publishing poetry, fiction and other literature mentioned in the previous chapter, and to introducing *new* authors to the world, are producing books that no ordinary book buyer will pay more than £1.00 for and may think overpriced at that; customers have a tendency to count the number of pages! Hence book-sellers will not normally stock home-produced books, certainly not the amateurishly finished jobs which form too large a proportion of the little-press output.

Fortunately booksellers, though harassed and impoverished, are by the nature of their calling civilised men and women; in the main extra-ordinarily nice people who want to promote books and literature, and who are often prepared to take small returns if everything else is made easy for them. If a small or 'independent' publisher can make friends with a bookseller, he can often get round him. There will be many book-sellers, and the buyers of big bookshops, who will not deign even to make an appointment. But it can be done here and there.

It should only be attempted where one's output makes sense; if one is issuing poetry, only a literary bookseller is worth approaching, and he will first bemoan the lack of public interest in poetry and point to the small shelf space he can allocate to it (every inch of shelving costs him in rent, rates and other overheads). If one is publishing fiction, it helps if the author has a 'name'. Charming little books on cookery, canals, veteran cars, cats (if illustrated), herbal cures and children may get tried out alongside the glossy products of commercial publishers cul-tivating these topics under the letter C. But the books must compete in visual appeal, a point we return to in Chapter 5.

Booksellers need to offer variety, indeed novelty, something new and even mildly controversial; the small publisher can offer unusual, even gimmicky, books which the bookseller thinks will catch his customers' fish-like eyes. He may try them as bait.

Many booksellers are forced to adopt other forms of retailing and services to make an income. (The sad fact is that the British public is still afraid of bookshops — it feels under-educated, under-bred and unhappy in the midst of the rows of titled spines, an air of bookishness and even erudition. This did not matter when the middle classes could keep bookshops going; today it does.) Some try to serve the local community in related ways, selling, for instance, tickets for local entertainments and displaying posters, perhaps dedicating a room to the meetings (including poetry readings) of local societies. Local societies imply local-interest publications on display, and that is an opening for the home publisher. If the local bookseller makes himself into a centre for communal activity, his friendship is invaluable.

Some bookshops specialise in stocking unusual and minority writing, or types of books, such as miniature books. Some who specialise in particular subjects — such as poetry or feminism or conservation — will take home-produced books (if competently produced) for completeness' sake in such lines. Some cover quite a range under the label 'alternative bookshops'. Seven or eight poetry bookshops exist, including that of the Poetry Society (21 Earls Court Square, London SW5.) which is subsidised (a receipt must be obtained for books accepted). All are choosy. Otherwise they might be overwhelmed by outpourings from the 'writing

Plate 7 Bernard Stone's Turret Bookshop, Lamb's Conduit Street, London WC1, which stocks private-press and little-press poetry books and similar items alongside 'trade' books

workshops'. They choose according to whether they think they can sell the author or the subject; their tastes and specialisms must be cultivated. It is senseless to offer Keats on hand-made paper to a shop specialising in contemporary verse forms. The Basilisk Press bookshop in Hampstead specialises in private-press books of high quality only, and it is pointless to offer such a shop typewriter settings of contemporary poets in stapled covers.

Even very large bookshop chains may be approached. Local-interest books (district guides, town histories, interesting walks etc) is the most likely line to get into local branches of W. H. Smith. But W. H. Smith informs us that any book will be considered if it is likely to attract publicity in the local press or radio. However it is necessary to approach such a huge concern as W. H. Smith in the prescribed way.

The home publisher should not expect to walk into a branch of Smiths and sell direct to the manager. If the book is likely to be of interest primarily in one branch, the manager should be asked the address of the Area Manager, to whom should be sent full details in writing, together with a copy (or advance copy) of the book. If for some reason the book is likely to find a market in widely separated branches, these details and the specimen copy should be sent to Retail Buying Division, Strand House, 10 New Fetter Lane, London EC4A 1AD. In either case, price, publication date, discount terms, and probable publicity (if known) should be mentioned. It is as well to approach W. H. Smith several weeks before publication, even if this means holding on to stock for a little while after finished copies are available, especially if Head Office has to be approached, in order to give time for any correspondence, and in certain instances distribution to several branches from the company's central warehouse.

Some booksellers, especially specialist ones, stipulate 'sale-or-return' terms. That is they pay the publisher only if they sell the copy: otherwise they return it at the publisher's expense — if they don't forget or are not reminded. It depends on the publisher whether he offers or accepts such terms, either for all his titles or perhaps for a special one. If he does, he must keep records.

Representation

Because the small publisher is his own rep (salesman) the number of booksellers he can cultivate is limited (though blessed is he whose wife is a born saleswoman). When he makes his time budget, he should consider how much time he will allocate to selling. We reckon that to *see* one bookseller takes on average half a day. Even so it is better to get one's books into two or three bookshops than into none. Many small publishers try to contract out the distribution of their books to a specialist firm. These exist, but they charge a stiffish subscription fee and take a 50 per cent mark up (out of which comes the bookseller's slice), and are only interested in a fair range of titles. They are not usually interested in a home publisher issuing small editions of two or three titles a year. They really cater for the small *commercial* publisher, and often offer warehousing and invoicing as well as delivery services.

What a home publisher really needs (especially if he works in the country) is a personal friend or two, particularly in London, who will, for love and maybe hospitality, do some representation for him. A few we know have such friends. Talk of small or private presses getting together to fund a 'rep' is endemic, but it never gets anywhere because by their nature home hobbyists cannot combine and the salary of a rep (a first-rate one may earn £12,000 a year or so with expenses) is too high anyway; even many commercial publishers have to share them. A possibility for moonlighting by the unemployed? Or by retired book enthusiasts? So far we have collected no examples.

It is always interesting to see what happens when one asks a friend who wants to order one's book to go to a bookshop for it. Frequently he is met with a flat refusal. He is told that the shop does not 'have an account' with the publisher and can only get books from publishers with whom it has an account. This is not true, but it derives from the bookseller's problems as we summarise them. The days when a tradesman advertised 'nothing is too much trouble' are over. Small publishers lose a lot of sales in this way.

The arts associations

The Arts Council and the regional arts associations receive taxpayers' money to encourage culture by subsidies; this includes literature but its share of the subsidy is small and was cut substantially in 1984. It has mainly been expended in subsidies to favoured publishers of poetry and kindred minority writing, and has therefore ended up mostly in the pockets of commercial printers since few of the recipient publishers do even a small part of their production themselves. The acknowledgement of this subsidy is a frank admission that such publications are non-viable, and in this sense the Council helps to fill the area which commercial publishers have vacated, as mentioned in Chapter 1.

This is legitimate as far as it goes, but it produces acrimony between benefactors and recipients. What one calls recognition of merit, the others — when their applications are rejected — call favouritism. This is always the result of subsidy in every field of national life and economics. Subsidies have certainly brought some semi-commercial

42

publishers with impressive imprints into being, and have helped several minor ones to keep afloat. It is perfectly simple for anyone to apply for a grant; the forms can be obtained from the local arts association. After that bureaucracy takes over. In our view, nobody should take up publishing and printing on the scale we discuss in this book in the hope of being subsidised by the taxpayer to do so. That will lead, not to the joys of publishing and craftsmanship, but to unhappiness.

It has always seemed to us a mistaken use of taxpayers' money to subsidise the production of books and periodicals rather than to develop markets in which the small publisher can expose his wares and ideas for sale — and let the public decide. We have made a strong plea for the bookseller, and we think that it is to the bookseller and distributor that the subsidies for literature and minority publishing should go. The bookseller, not the printing trade, is the pillar of our national culture which is most in need of the Arts Council's support. It is time that the difficulties booksellers face and the service to the arts and to education they render should be recognised.

Some time ago we submitted proposals for a scheme to effect this redistribution of state and local-government subsidy. Under it, the arts associations would hire shelf space from booksellers (much as some paperback publishers do) on which small-press publications would be stocked on the usual discount terms to the bookseller. He would receive the rental (which would take his overheads into account) and the discount for books sold, like any other book, which he would hold on sale-or-return terms. After a period the publishers of unsold books would be notified to collect them, and others substituted. In this way, the public would decide, and the problem of accumulations of shop-soiled amateur books would be avoided. The incentive would be placed squarely on the minority publisher, to produce attractive-looking books that would sell — of course participation in the scheme would not inhibit him from selling in every other way he could.

It is an encouraging development that local arts associations are operating or testing variations of this idea, which accord with Sir William Rees Mogg's policy of diverting Arts Council resources from the metropolis to the regions. The best-established of such schemes is that of the Yorkshire Arts Association, which has been in operation successfully for ten years. It varies in some respects from ours, but does aim at paying the bookseller. Under this scheme the Association buys outright a certain number of copies of all — or almost all — the minority publications (books and periodicals) issued in its area. It supplies a specially designed rack to booksellers, now over seventy, in the scheme, and they receive the whole price of the books sold from the rack. The Association maintains a part-time worker who supervises the racks, visiting the

Plate 8 The Yorkshire Arts Association distribution scheme for Yorkshire independent presses and magazines: 70 bookshops display this rack of publications (*Graham Sykes*)

44

booksellers, and replenishing stocks; unsold items are either pulped or sold as remainders at book fairs.

In effect this scheme gives the small publishers a basic 'subscription list' for their output which covers bare costs; it is up to them to top up these receipts by selling elsewhere. The Association decides what quantities to buy and is experienced in what will 'go' and what will linger, and buys accordingly. It claims that the scheme shows the public will buy minority literature. Nor is the scheme hard on the ratepayer — it costs less than £5,000 a year (see Plate 8).

Other regional arts associations take a different line. Some, like Eastern Arts and South-West Arts, run bookshops of their own. Others, notably Greater London, encourage and subsidise local community associations to run bookshops, organise writers' and poets' 'workshops', and to publish local work. They give preference to their own locals, but usually accept any minority publications, on sale-or-return terms. The Arts Council approves, because it regards such activity as 'therapy' for the underdog and the unemployed, rather than as literature for which their own often generous donations are reserved. This attitude is resented at the lower level. However, one productive way in which both levels could co-operate would be to use some of the money in providing the reps for small publishers and little presses which, as noted above, they cannot individually afford. Based on a regional council such a rep could get quite a lot of good work into bookshops, theatre kiosks and other unconventional retail outlets.

The sales made by some of the community bookshops are impressive. Centreprise, which runs a bookshop-reading room-cafeteria-workshop in Hackney had sponsored (up to 1979) some forty publications, and brings out five a year. It claims sales of up to 10,000 for some of these. The emphasis is on the East London area, naturally, and a certain political inclination is detectable. Its own books are well displayed along with 'Trade' books and Open University textbooks which ensure a flow of custom. But for Centreprise, run as a co-operative, the area would have *no* bookshop.

The home publisher does well to ascertain the acceptability of his books at any such community bookshop in his area. But such activities can never take the place of normal bookshop exposure.

Other retail outlets

Other ways of selling books exist, particularly if the subject is specialised. The time-honoured method is the subscription list. If the would-be home publisher personally knows the book buyers or collectors who are interested, he can circularise them all and produce an edition tailored to that market. Nancy Cunard did know them, and Bloomsbury knew her; some of her books were sold out before they were bound. Booksellers who have an interest in publishing are well-placed to operate this way. They know from experience roughly what will sell and to whom. Being over-busy men they normally have their books commercially printed (unless they patronise a private press with exacting standards). Such a venture was Mr Bernard Stone's Turret Books.

Otherwise a subscription list must be worked up over a period. This is a matter of the quality of the books themselves — quality in matter or content, and almost certainly both. If, for example, a small press gets the work of well-known names in the poetry scene, the *cognoscenti* of poetry will usually put in a standing order for all titles as they appear. The publisher then can cover most of his out-of-pocket costs from his subscription-list sales; other sales help his overheads.

Building up a subscription list is another aspect of building an imprint: a choice of good authors, good (however offbeat) writing, good and recognisable format and presswork, and regular (not necessarily large) production over a number of years.

Poetry readings probably generate the greatest sale of books of poetry. At these the author can display and sell his books (perhaps signed copies) to members of the audience. Engagements to read are an indication of his standing, since most readings are now subsidised by the regional arts associations, who are even being forced to pay a substantial fee — £50 in 1983. Many well-established small publishers make sure their author is in the magic circuit of poetry readings. The selection of poets and the organisation of readings is a major function of the Poetry Society in London; but there are many others, and some freelance organisers. The Society will always oblige with advice.

For other kinds of literature — for example local history — there is no comparable exposure. However, for local history and topography the local museums and libraries are often an outlet; some now run bookstalls. Such work interests local conservation and research societies who organise talks (and walks). Moreover, gift (and kitsch) shops will often stock books on these subjects when they would stock no others: especially illustrated books, with reproductions of old photographs and postcards.

Publicity

It is possible to advertise, as commercial publishers do, if on a small scale. Anyone thinking of laying out money in this way should consider the experienced, and even jaundiced, views of commercial publishers on this subject. Few regard advertising as a way of winning sales. They think of it as a necessity to *announce* a title (and therefore think primarily of *The Bookseller*) and secondarily to promote the goodwill of their imprint generally. They never advertise to push a flagging sale; they regard advertising as a whip to speed an already-spinning top. It is when a book is selling well — and so getting mouth-to-ear recommendation — that they take space in the literary journals and the Sunday 'qualities'; or, if a specialised book, in the specialised press.

The small man can take the same line, using the modestly priced space of the small magazines, and the weekly book page of the local paper (if, amazingly, it has one). *The Times Literary Supplement* has a moderately priced classified-ads column designed to attract small and offbeat publishers' announcements.

The Association of Little Presses issues an annual catalogue of little-press publications in which a page or half-page can be taken cheaply — and helps the Association, which has somehow forfeited its grant from the Arts Council, to survive. *British Book News,* which is taken by librarians and book-buyers, specialises in 'small ads' for small editions and 'press books'.

Reviews and publicity may be considered together. If a book has any sort of a 'news angle' it is only sense for the publisher and author to try to interest the local press in it. The 'personalised' feature article, or the 'review article', is better publicity than a review or mention in the review section. There is everything to be said for preparing a 'hand-out' to ease the journalist's task, nor is it much trouble. Better still to know the editor of the local paper or of the journal 'most likely to'. Such publicity-seeking mirrors in miniature exactly what large publishers keep a whole department to do, and they rarely miss a trick. It places a corresponding burden on the one-man show.

Authors assume that reviews, like advertisements, sell books. Most publishers deny it, though they like reviews, indeed solicit them by every means possible; and, like advertisements, good reviews are regarded as a boost for sales. Some authors, especially poets, are more interested in reviews than sales — they wish to impress the in-group. Reviews have a limited effect, though we know of exceptions to this rule. A good review of a small edition in a first-rate journal is bound to help sales just because the total edition is so small — whereas a response of 25 buyers is negligible to Oxford University Press. It is a big lift to a small press. However, the home publisher suffers from the drawback that, when one gets the review, the copies may not be in the relevant bookshops; worse, their existence may be hotly denied and an alternative title assiduously pushed. In the second place, reviews of small-press titles have become more rare; partly because they are limited editions, and hand-printed. The editor is instinctively against them.

47

A publisher we know had a dozen copies of a beautiful hand-printed book, which he intended to retail in paper covers, specially bound in hardback for reviewers. He got not one mention, and felt aggrieved. We, who have seen the 'Trade' books for review piled up like tower blocks in literary-editors' offices, and have noticed the growing press view that reviews are not news and so deserve less and less space, were saddened but not surprised by his story. A lot of review copies will be simply wasted; that is the name of the game — worse, they will be re-sold, unreviewed, if they have residual value to the review department of the paper. The author should be asked to make a list of the reviewers he knows personally and is prepared to grovel to; and that should be the greater part of the review list. When it works — success is sweet!

The same caution should be observed in attempting direct-mail advertising for small editions. If the possible subscribers are few, an announcement by post is the answer; but otherwise the returns are unlikely to balance the cost of postage and stationery at current rates. As a list of subscribers and enquirers is built up, 'fliers' can be sent out, and in any event the small publisher needs his 'list' of books in print just as the large publisher does; and it can be an interesting as well as inexpensive item. Ingenuity is needed to prevent such material from going the way of all 'junk mail'. But the economics of a large-scale campaign are against all book publishers, even big ones. The postage alone at 13p a time is £10 for 80 shots, £31 for 240 shots, £130 for 1,000 shots — and a thousand is peanuts unless it is to an extremely well-selected mailing-list. Some booksellers will, for a fee, insert fliers into their mailed lists.

An easier method than co-operating to pay a rep would be for home publishers to combine in compiling such a mailing list, and sharing the postage of covers containing announcements of new titles and lists of books in print. Unfortunately such proposals, as we have seen, have broken down on the individualism of publishers. Such individualism is at once their raison d'être and their downfall.

There are other ways of selling books. In Covent Garden we met an engaging character with an American accent asking passers-by if they were interested in poetry. If they were (we were) he offered a collection of his own for 50p — and this was a mere gathering of A4 typed sheets stapled into a coloured cover. He had it printed for him, he said, and otherwise had no expenses beyond shoe leather, making a modest income out of street sales in big cities from San Francisco to Moscow. Some pertinacious community presses practise successful door-to-door salesmanship — they dispose of adequate 'person power' to do so.

Toni Savage, of Leicester, established a firm foundation for his press by printing programmes and folders for the local folk theatre: over 245 broadsheets have subsequently flowed from his press, which has become a local institution.

The public responds to unorthodox approaches, and it is part of the challenge of home publishing to think of ways of promoting one's creations that cut through mainstream methods.

The collectors

Through this review of outlets for small editions runs the thread of collectors' interests. As is known, people will collect anything from birds' eggs to manhole covers. It is hard to think of any object that is not collected. Collecting is a component of the human psyche, normal or not-so-normal. Book collecting antedates the printed book.

However, book collecting is not an easy market to survey. Suffice it to say that every aspect of a book or booklet is collected by somebody; even ephemera — collectors have asked for our fliers and lists *only*. In the main it is authors that are collected, and this generates demands for small editions of bibliographies for the printing of which some presses have been set up exclusively.

No less pertinaciously, illustrators, illustrations, and illustrated books are collected and also give rise to bibliographies and catalogues. Artists' values go up when they die. Of course fashions are capricious. And poor stuff does not get off the ground, besides spoiling a book's appearance. Scruffy, slapdash graffiti from inefficient art schools is best left to the periodical market.

Bindings are collected. Bookplates *in situ* are collected. First editions, any sort of 'first' by an author later famous, are eagerly sought out.

The work of the private presses, the so-called 'press books', constitute several markets. There are the out-of-print books from the 'classical' private presses, like Morris' Kelmscott editions, the work of the Vale, Eragny, Ashendene and other presses. This market need not be discussed here. The tradition of such luxury editions is today followed by such modern exemplars as the Whittington Press, operated by the Randles in Gloucestershire and the Tern Press run by the Parrys in Shropshire. The commercial replacement of letterpress printing by litho-offset techniques will make the collection of hand-printed books of the highest craftsmanship a speciality. Such presses virtually publish only for the lovers of 'fine printing'; they are adepts in the finer points of typography and letterpress technique, the use of hand-made paper and luxury binding. Sheer craftsmanship can thus form the material of a prosperous business, with a large export potential. The practical sections of this book, however, must be regarded as a mere introduction to such up-market bookmanship.

49

Plate 9 The home-publisher's 'list': a few of the attractive book announcements put out by little presses and private presses. These are from Moss Rose, Brewhouse, Leopard's Head, Morrigu, Melissa, Fantome presses, and a 'flier' of Ralph Chubb's. Some serve as broadsheets as well as adverts

Fortunately, however, the books from more unassuming presses are also collected; prices are lower, but scarcity value ensures that they go up. Books of ours, originally put out at five shillings a copy in the Sixties, now startle us in secondhand-book-dealers' catalogues priced at ten to twenty pounds and more. Such an accretion of value, however, depends less on 'fine printing' (which is often absent) than on the subsequent fame of the author and artist, or on the reputation of the press, or on the subject of the text itself. The wind bloweth where it listeth.

Collectors do not ignore books published for other purposes by means of the newer technologies. This is a matter of author and subject. We have an American friend who, for ten years, collected as much of the 'way out' and 'beatnik' ephemera put out in the vintage years of protest as he could. Much of it, given away, he got for nothing; but he set up a small fund to buy six copies of anything for sale in this field, without regard to quality or content. When he came to catalogue this mass of material (he is a librarian with a sideline book business) he found the job would take him too long and decided to sell it uncatalogued. What had cost him about $5,000 was bought by a bookseller determined to have the finest collection of the poetry of protest in the world, for some $30,000.

But for the home publisher this is not a market easily found, easily as it will absorb a collectable item when it *is* found. There are directories of book-collectors, for example the directory published by the Sheppards from Trigram Press. The membership lists of the Private Libraries Association also list collectors' interests. These are useful, but naturally depend on the readiness of collectors to provide information and addresses; they are far from being comprehensive. The problem resolves itself into the basic one of publicity. Getting one's books known, into catalogues of any sort, is well worth while. A wide reading of the press, especially the correspondence columns, is a useful auxiliary in compiling one's own list of 'prospects' for circularising. It is also possible to buy mailing lists — like that of the Booksellers' Association. The cost is likely to be higher than the return; here DIY applies — draw up your own list, and supplement it from other sources. (A home-publisher's list may well be headed by rich Aunt Adelaide!) Sadly, authors that a home publisher has sweated blood to publish all too rarely buy his subsequent books by *other* authors.

Libraries, including university and academic libraries, are by definition collectors. But the library trade is a difficult one. One's local library may or may not take hand-printed books from locals — or even trade books from local authors. Ours, for example, do *not*. But a friend finds a ready sale for his history monographs in his neighbourhood library. Universities often collect particular authors, and especially poets. Their librarians are worth circularising. A few actually specialise in small editions. (All libraries prefer hardback bindings.)

Self-evidently, Scottish libraries are interested in Scottish authors and subjects, and Welsh libraries in the culture of Wales. Reference books about universities and their specialities are worth consulting (though professors, readers and research units are deluged with junk mail). Specialist libraries have their own interests even in the small-press field, and can be consulted through their association, ASLIB.

Commercial publishers hold book fairs, of which the summit is the annual Frankfurt fair; mostly such fairs are used by big buying organisations. The smaller commercial publishers, and even the private presses, have their own annual fair in London. The cost of a small table is not prohibitive if shared by a co-operating group of small imprints who between them can put up an interesting display of titles. The home publisher, however, should see in it an occasion for socialising, learning from others, and having fun, rather than for substantial sales. Simply as an entertainment it may be worth the entrance fee. Some good bookshops hold book fairs, for example David's bookshop in Letchworth, Hertfordshire.

The book fairs put on by other bodies, like the Association of Little

Presses, or, more ambitiously, the Cambridge Poetry Festival, are rarely commercial successes for publishers, as opposed to authors paid to read at them. They are often subsidised by regional arts associations as shop windows for their 'literature workshops' and so forth, but the difficulty of luring the general public inside has yet to be overcome. Still, they too are usually good fun.

Extraordinary as it may appear, quite substantial and successful trade publishers will ruefully confide that they have no exact idea how they sell books at all. Yet they survive. So small and amateur publishers should never be discouraged. We know a few home publishers — usually self-publishers at that — who take almost no steps to announce, advertise or distribute their productions, yet, sitting in their chairs at home, sell up to 300 copies of each title by orders arriving through the post. They have a knack: their publications are somehow unusual and intriguing. Recommendation by word of mouth has a great and unquantifiable amount to do with the selling of books, including small and limited editions.

Just as the problem of representation in the home market is difficult, so too is the problem of representation abroad — which mainly means in the United States. Book-distribution firms advertise their services in *The Bookseller* and other trade journals. The first rule is the giving of very large discounts on rather inflated prices, and the second is having a regular throughput of titles — for otherwise they lose interest. To celebrate the 1976 US bicentennial one of us published an unknown and previously unpublished poem by the eighteenth-century notable, Charles Wesley, brother of John, on the American revolutionary war. It was (and is) unique. By the time — about a year later — the American universities wanted copies, it was out of print.

The range of possibilities is wide, and the home publisher should trawl them all. We can give but a selection of the resources to be tapped in the Appendix.

Publication rites and rights

There are certain preliminaries to the publishing and distribution of any book which we have left till last. By law, both the publisher's and the printer's name and address must appear inside the book (see page 102); some self-publishers forget this though few have been fined or confined to the Tower as yet. It is, however, absurd to leave out the publisher's address since it is an advertisement both of his activities and a source whence copies may be obtained.

Furthermore, every title should be given an International Standard Book Number, the so-called 'ISBN' which is printed on the title verso and at the bottom of the front flap of the jacket (or on the back of a paperback). This enables the title to be identified easily by librarians and booksellers. It is in four parts, as will be exemplified if the reader who is unfamiliar with the system turns to the verso of the title-page of this book, where its ISBN is printed: 0 7153 8510 0. The first part identifies the book as published in the UK (France uses the identifier 2). The second group of digits identifies a specific publisher, in this case, David & Charles Ltd. The third group identifies the title or edition on the publisher's list. The fourth is a device called a digit check, which checks against errors in the intermediate figures. Any publisher, even a self-publisher, can obtain the appropriate number for his title(s) without charge from the Standard Book Numbering Agency, 12 Dyott Street, London WC1A 1DF, who will readily explain the system in more detail if this is required.

A similar system exists to identify periodicals and part-publications — a series of numbered poem cards is an example — by means of an International Standard Serials Number. The scheme is operated by the UK National Serials Data Centre at the British Library, 2 Sheraton Street, London W1V 4BH; they will supply a 'data sheet' to applicants and explain the system.

J. Whitaker & Sons Ltd (also at 12 Dyott Street, London WC1A 1DF) provide publishers, even the smallest, with yellow publication announcement forms for new titles, details from which are then inserted into *The Bookseller*'s weekly list of new publications, into *Books of the Month,* and finally into the important annual record, *British Books in Print.* This preliminary move should never be omitted.

The law requires that a copy of every book — widely defined — must be sent free to the Copyright Receipt Office of the British Library (2 Sheraton Street, London W1V 4BH). Compliance is advisable, because a receipt is sent and the title should duly appear in the British National Bibliography, published weekly with interim and annual cumulations. Frequently a title from a home publisher does *not,* but one is entitled to badger the British Library until it *does.* As a result of that entry many foreign orders may be obtained, especially from American and Commonwealth libraries, who may be buying by author's name.

Unfortunately the law also requires that five other libraries are entitled to free copies. Four of these (the university libraries of Oxford and Cambridge, the National Library of Scotland, and Trinity College Library, Dublin, which was once the second capital of the Empire but is now capital of a foreign state) demand a copy through their agent at 100 Euston Street, London NW1 2HQ. The fifth, the National Library of Wales, is only entitled to a copy if it applies direct to the publisher. None of these libraries, amassing valuable collections, pays a penny for the privilege, and they do nothing whatsoever to help the small or home publisher, or the private presses. It is a scandal. What a pleasure it is to serve a non-statutory university library.

The Library of Congress, Washington DC, no longer issues catalogue numbers to British publications, but it is grateful for gifts, catalogues them, and is a worthwhile recipient for certain titles.

The other self-evident preliminary to publishing is a system, however simple, of records (see page 182).

4

BUYING AND PLANNING PRINT

'Having it printed'

This chapter is intended as an introductory guide to those who might like to set up as a small publisher, but cannot consider undertaking any part of the production process at home.

It might seem that if this is the idea, it is unnecessary to do more than find a commercial printer, the cheaper the better. We have met many well-intentioned people who supposed that buying print was as straightforward as buying the services of a carpenter or house painter. It is not so. The previous chapter should have indicated that even books in small editions have to be tailored to markets in appearance and presentation. It is enough to walk round a general bookshop to realise this. Even standard novels vary in size, format, typography and binding. Book jackets are as lushly varied as a tropical scene. In the children's section the books will range from very large to very small in size — what's the reason? It may be assumed that there is a good reason — each is aimed at a particular part of the 'kiddiliterature' market and designed and priced accordingly. Paperbacks may seem to vary little — until one looks inside them with a critical eye.

Under the pressure of competition commercially produced and marketed books are designed to be as cheaply produced and priced as possible — and this goes for the most lavishly got-up art books. The 'unit cost of production' which is the total printing and binding bill divided by the number of copies in the edition is not the selling cost, which must cover publishers' overheads, booksellers' margins and so on. The unit cost becomes an ever-smaller part of the total selling cost as the edition increases. For an edition of 3,000 copies of a 128-page hardback book the unit cost might be £1.00, while the book is priced at £4.95 or even £5.95 to cover all the other costs of publishing it. If the book sells well, and the second printing is 30,000 copies, the unit cost would fall to 45–50p. If this book started as a paperback and became a best seller, the unit cost might fall to 15p for 300,000 copies. A publisher sure of sales of 50,000 is less worried about cutting unit costs than if he can only sell 3,000.

55

The publisher of small editions is therefore very concerned about slicing pennies off his unit and total costs. He has to pay much the same printing costs for his small edition of 500 as the commercial publisher for his 3,000, perhaps a little less, as he is saving on paper, but perhaps more since he is less experienced in buying print and has insufficient overall volume to qualify for concessionary reductions.

He needs therefore to choose every process in the making of his books with an eye to economy yet without prejudicing their appearance and sales appeal. He needs, at the outset, to get estimates from more than one printer, to insist that they are set out in reasonable detail, and to understand them. His understanding of the printers' estimates is vital to his confidence that when the copies are delivered they will correspond exactly to what he wants. Professional publishers do know this, or their production managers know it for them. If one doesn't know, one is liable to get something rather different from what publisher and author had in mind. Our earlier observations on self-publishing are pertinent here.

What follows is also relevant to the publisher who intends to cut his costs by doing some of the production at home. Only by understanding commercial print-buying can he know which process to 'buy out', and which to do 'in house' by himself: what is within his competence and what is not. The study of book-making and book-design properly begins with an examination of dealings with printers.

Furthermore, no matter how often one goes to a tried and trusted printer, every contract should be re-examined to see if costs can be cut further, if only because labour-saving or other cost-saving changes in technology follow one another so fast nowadays.

Stages in making a book

Getting a book printed today is almost certainly a matter of having it printed by offset-litho. The number of letterpress printers, or printers who operate both letterpress and offset-litho equipment is dwindling. The difference in method should, even so, be understood.

Letterpress has for 500 years meant the direct inking of surfaces in raised relief, assembled in the past by hand, but from the 1890s mechanically assembled from individual letters that are cast separately on the Monotype system, or in single solid lines called 'slugs' by the Linotype ('line-of-type') machine — paper is then pressed against the inked surface. The difference between the systems is shown by the fact that when making corrections, Monotype-cast letters can be changed individually, whereas the correction of a single letter in Linotype-cast matter requires the re-setting of the entire line. However the time involved and therefore the cost is much the same. Composition of newspapers used always to be by Linotype because slugs are quicker to arrange on the 'stone' (the flat imposition surface), while books were mostly 'comped' by Monotype (in Britain, anyway). Prior to mechanical setting, all books were composed by hand from 'case', letter by letter; now the hand-setting of texts (as opposed to 'display') is relegated almost wholly to private presses.

The first cost in 'buying out print' in the form of letterpress, or any other form, is the cost of composition, or setting, or, as we shall now usually call it for convenience, 'origination'. The term is mostly used in the Trade for converting to film, but has come to be applied — to suit the procedures of the new printing processes — to the preparation of both text and 'graphics' (pictures, tabular matter, maps, ornament) combined. Very broadly, in the letterpress process, illustration is limited to 'line blocks' for reproducing line drawings in black and white, or in colour, and 'half-tone blocks' for reproducing the tones and shades of photographs (explained fully in Chapter 10). These blocks are still expensive, around £1.00 per square inch for zinc line blocks and £2.00 per square inch for half-tones.

In the letterpress process, type and blocks are assembled in pages ('imposed'); proofs are pulled, and, after corrections, the whole is locked up into steel 'chases' (frames) in the proper order for printing. Obviously, corrections take time and cost money. The buyer of print knows well that if the typescript ('the copy') is *perfect,* and not even a letter is changed from this original by the author's second thoughts, corrections cost nothing on the actual final bill, as the printer undertakes to put right his own errors. He knows that he will make some, and lose time, so he makes allowance for this when he quotes for composition, or origination, of the text (and graphics, if any). All manuscripts or typescripts should be 'clean copy'. Corrections are unavoidable, even massive, in the texts and proofs of newspapers and some periodicals; hence their very high origination cost.

It is unnecessary here to describe the presses used to do the machining. Commercially this is likely to be done on large 'flatbed' machines in which the paper is caught between rollers and rolled against the type on the bed. The cost of machining is made up of preparation for the run, which may be heavy, and of the run itself which is a matter only of time, supervision and electricity. Flatbed machines used to be used for all runs of about 5,000 impressions taken. So, if the run is only 200, the heavy preparation costs must show up in the disproportionately high 'unit cost' of the book.

The paper for the run is charged separately as it varies according to the quality specified (see Chapter 11).

Next comes the folding of the sheets (usually of eight pages on each side of the sheet), also done by machine, in their correct order, and 'gathering', and the process of binding them into covers, with which we deal later. These stages comprise 'finishing', and form another item on the bill.

If one can find a printer still using letterpress his tender may be the lowest because he is using written-down equipment which he does not intend to replace, while his offset-litho competitor is still paying for his.

The up-to-date printer using offset-lithography will originate the typescript either on an IBM composer (a elaborate kind of typewriter with an electronic memory and controls) or on a sophisticated photo-setting machine. Either way the printer will supply 'galley proofs' for correction.

The offset-litho firm has now to prepare the corrected galley (or page) proofs, and insert the graphics (Chapter 10) as required for the book. For the graphics there are no block charges, but the printer charges for the origination process, including process camera work, etc. He makes plates from the completed artwork with the correct page sequence, attaches these to his offset machine and prints.

Paper charges will be the same, and so will the charge for the finishing processes.

'Finishing' a book by a commercial printer will prove a heavy item on the estimate. It will depend on the customer's choice of method. A paper-back with a square spine either sewn by machine or 'perfect bound' (ie glued to the spine by a modern adhesive, as in a cheap commercial paperback) will naturally cost more than a merely stapled booklet using wire staples (eventually to rust unpleasantly). For longish runs, a perfect-bound commercial paperback costs about 12p to bind per copy, and 35p for a sewn binding to card covers. Hardback binding ('case-bound') is 80p to £1.00 per copy in cloth; it *can* cost £5 to £20 a copy.

There is also the cost of the bookjacket which protects the hardback cover (the same design may be used for the paperback cover if there is also a paperback edition). The customer buying his book from a printer will find buying and fitting a jacket for short runs of 200–500 very expensive. It is costly for commercial books too — it may amount to as much as half the total cost of binding the book in an edition of 5,000.

Some examples of estimates

These are the processes whose costs the publisher can check if he can get detailed estimates. Small printers, however, grudge the time spent in itemising their estimates. Large printers are rarely interested in small editions or runs. Nevertheless the buyer of print must persevere. Without estimates he is lost.

Printing costs are continually rising, if not as much as they did. Between 1977 and 1981 they rose by 7½ to 10 per cent a year, but they are now down to about 2–3 per cent. We can only give prices 'as of 1983', and readers should add the current rate of inflation to the sample costings given below. They are from well-established book printers who will produce a professional looking book. Book printing, as opposed to other printing, is a specialist job, and commercial publishers tend to ring the changes on only three or four; in all, there are probably less than fifty with first-class reputations.

Unemployment has produced a crop of cut-price printshops run by former craftsmen, but these, for reasons given later, cannot design a book, only follow instructions. A publisher who cannot give such instructions is put to the extra expense of paying a designer, who will charge £50 to £100 to design a simple book; it *can* cost far more.

However there is also a growing number of small-booklet specialists in the provinces whose prices would be keener than those given below. When approaching any such printer, one should always ask to see specimens of work done.

Let us take two fairly typical small-press booklets, one of 32 pages and the other of 48 pages. The technical specifications to the printer of the first-mentioned are as follows: size, 216 x 138mm (ie metric demy 8vo — see Chapter 11 on book sizes); 32 pages, black only. Setting in 10-point type, following marked-up copy; one set page proofs before printing; make plates on approval and print 300 copies (with 200 run-on) on 100gsm white antique laid paper (see Chapter 11 for these terms) supplied by printer. Show running sheets before finishing for approval. Cover from same-size line artwork to be supplied by printer; printer to make blocks/plates and print in one colour on 200gsm art board pages 1 and 4 only. Binding to be sheets folded to suitable imposition and saddle stitched with two wires, trimmed, and packed in parcels, 25 copies per parcel. Delivery and schedule dates for proofs to be specified. Payment terms: 50 per cent on acceptance of order, balance on delivery one month.

ESTIMATE	£
Setting 26pp @ £6 per page	156
Litho plate-making	80
Paper ex-printer as specified	21
Print 300	28
Cover — print and board cost	26
Finishing	30
(Run-on 200 copies, £50 extra)	341

On this basis, the unit cost of an edition of 300 is £1.14 per copy, for 500, 80p per copy. The estimate for printing the book by a letterpress printer was, in this case, much the same. No cost for plates, but the machining cost rose to £40 and the cost of making line blocks for the illustrations to print with the text was an extra £35. The saving by using letterpress was thus £20 only.

Printed at home, the out-of-pocket expenses of this booklet amounted only to £35 for blocks, paper, covers and sundries; the copies, further, were sewn not stapled, and the cover was an elegant wrapper with a printed spine for which the printer could not quote at all. These out-of-pocket expenses, of course, do not take into consideration the original purchase prices of the press, type, etc. (which are spread over a succession of titles) or the owner's time.

The second example was a title printed similarly as to size and quality of paper, but called for 48 pages in three sections to be thread-sewn, with a 'drawn-on' cover (ie one with a printed square spine) printed in two colours from artwork supplied, on 240gsm board.

ESTIMATE	£
Setting 40pp @ £6 per page	240
Litho plate-making	120
Paper supplied ex printer	28
Print 300	42
Cover — print and board cost	45
Finishing	381
(Run-on cost per 200, £120)	856

These figures are worth consideration. The high cost of finishing (binding and associated processes) strikes the eye. The reason lies in the number of operations to crease and fold the board, and the sewing of the three 16-page sections (probably by hand) to glue into the cover so formed, probably by an outside binder. Thus the estimated unit cost was £2.86 per copy for 300 and £1.95 for 500. If the book had been printed by letterpress, the estimate was £90 less.

The out-of-pocket cost for the actual printing at home of this booklet was about £100, and this included the cost of subcontracting the printing of the cover to an 'instant' printer by offset-litho. The addition of a second colour to the cover design, and the creasing of the cover, was done at home. The unit cost of the 400 copies was thus actually little over 25p, and the retail price was set at £2.25.

The high cost of originating both booklets by a professional printer stands out. In quoting £6 per page, the printers were including the artwork and 'paste-up' involved when the text is set by composer or photosetting machine, or, if the text is set in metal type, origination included imposition of type, blocks etc.

If one buys in only galley-proofs of photoset copy, or of Linotype slugs to print from on one's own machine, the cost per page in 1983 averaged £3.50 to £4.50.

These two examples were of books of poetry; how much does it cost to bring out a book with a substantial text — say 50,000 words? We give two estimates for the printing of such a book, 128 pages of straight prose setting, without illustrations and bound sewn into a card cover ('academic paperback' style), 500 copies. Printer No 1 estimated £880 for setting eight 16-page sections and printing by offset-litho, £100 for two-colour cover, and 30p for binding; total cost £1,300 approximately, unit cost £2.26 per copy.

Printer No 2 offered a better-quality job at a total cost of £1,430, unit cost about £2.86 (down to £1.75 for 1,000 copies). He quoted typeset and layout (origination) at £780; plates, paper and board at £270, and he grouped printing, binding and trimming for a sum of £380. These two estimates show the difficulty of comparing two printers — but also provide a rule of thumb for costing a prose book — from £10 to £12 per page.

Even before a printer can put in his estimates he must have a specification as in the two poetry books — size of page, type of binding, etc; and a *design*. Without a design he will 'design' the book himself, deciding the margins, length of line, title page layout and so on.

The printer who is used only to turning out social and business stationery, invitations, etc, will reveal his ignorance of book design if left to his own devices. The old craft printers could design fine books. The rise of the typographer has changed that. Bruce Rogers, the famous American typographer and typophile, admitted that he hated all contact with the composing room or machine room at his printers; and today designers are men of the drawing-board and VDU only. This means that the modern printer is like a builder — he works only to definite instructions. If he does not get them he holds up production until he does — or he guesses. The cost, in time and errors, is for the customer's account.

It follows, therefore, that the 'print buyer' must understand book design and how to 'mark up' the 'copy' (see Fig 4). The only alternative to becoming something of a designer is either to pay a designer or to give the printer a comparable book as a model and specify 'exactly like that'. A *first-rate* printer will ensure that it is exactly like.

The advantage of becoming one's own designer, on the other hand, is that one can design with an eye to economy at every stage. Design should be conceived with the printer and his resources, and with one's own resources, in mind throughout. This is dealt with in the next chapter.

Preparing the manuscript

Before preparing the design, the manuscript itself must be edited and assessed; for its length and content, and any inclusion of graphics, dictate much of the design. The first procedure is to cast off the typescript to find the number of words. The method chosen depends on the typescript. If the pages are pretty regular, with the same number of lines per page and roughly the same length of line, it is simple to count the number of lines, multiply by the number of pages, and the whole by the average words per line. This will certainly do for short texts in most cases.

A more exact method is to draw a line down the right-hand margin of the same distance as the shortest line per page (but ignoring paragraph endings). The total number of words and characters within that line can be calculated (see below) quite easily and then the number of characters and words on each page that extend beyond it can be also easily totted up and added to the total.

Some manuscripts are still handwritten. It is essential to have them re-typed if intended for a printer. The home printer may work from a short handwritten MS. Every word on the page must then be counted, the number noted and the total totted up.

A character count is more accurate than a word count when the stage comes of deciding how many printed pages the copy is to occupy. This involves deciding the length of the line in type ('the measure'), the size of type (number of lines per page), even the typeface, as some typefaces 'get in' more words than others. The calculation becomes more complex if allowance must be made for footnotes in a smaller type size, and for graphics or other features that break up the type areas and must be added to the total of pages needed. If there are chapter heads or gaps between sections of matter, these must be allowed for. Finally, there must be added in the pages for the title page and so forth, as shown in the next chapter.

If the intention is only to use a typewriter to originate the text for offset-litho reproduction, the calculation is fairly simple: the printed text will correspond closely to the typescript copy, adjusting the words per page of the one against the other (ie, if a foolscap typescript is to be reproduced as a quarto or octavo booklet).

It will also be a simple calculation if a typescript is to be originated for the book by means of an IBM composer, where there is no justification of the right-hand margin. But where a true typographical typeface is used, for either the offset-litho or letterpress process, the position is different, because a line of typewriting is not equivalent to a line of true typography.

Typographic measurement: points, picas, inches

Type measurements are based on a module of 72 points to an inch (see pp 89–91). Six lines to an inch depth on a page involves using a type body size of 12 points. 10-point type permits just over seven lines to the inch depth, and so on until a 6-point type allows 12 lines to the inch depth — a size usually confined to bibles, footnotes and the small print on the back of hire-purchase contracts.

The number of words that can be got into a line varies with each typeface; but handy tables exist to enable one to work this out. For the home book designer the simplest plan is to have a typescale, like a graduated ruler but in points, to measure the size of type in a book on his shelves comparable to the one he is designing and to count the words it makes per line or per page (see Fib 12).

So armed, the designer has the first element of his specification to the printer: the number of pages at so many lines per page. He takes the total number of characters (on average a word in English consists of six characters including the space between it and the next word — but call it seven for a scientific text) and he divides this total by the number of characters in a page of the chosen length:

$$\frac{\text{Total no of characters (6 x no of words)}}{\text{lines per page x characters per line of y ems}}$$

(an 'em' is one sixth of an inch, known as a 'pica' em).

An example would be this: 1,500 words equals 9,000 characters. The line measurement is 3 inches (18 ems) and the typeface chosen, say Plantin, yields an average of 13 characters per inch, or 39 per 3-inch line. So,

$$\frac{9{,}000}{36 \text{ (lines per page) x 39 (characters per line)}} = 7 \text{ pages}$$

Now, since pages are printed in multiples of four, the designer knows that he needs an 8-page pamphlet to incorporate a text of that length in 12-point type. If that does not suit him, he can add pages by increasing the size of type, and/or shortening the 'measure' (length of line), adding running heads to the pages and adopting other designers' tricks for 'driving out the matter'. And similarly in reverse if the text has to be crammed into fewer pages.

It is hard to see the fun of being a home publisher blessed with enough money to pay outside printers to do the hard work, without at least learning to design one's own books and leave the stamp of one's own style upon them. Designing is no sort of a mystery. It can be self-taught. The models are on every bookshelf. With a typescale or ruler to measure the size of pages and margins and the width and depths of texts anyone can analyse the proportions and style that give comeliness to a given book. Such tactical exercises without troops will teach a would-be publisher (and a publisher dissatisfied with his products) a great deal; but there are very worthwhile manuals on the subject to be consulted also (see Bibliography).

In this book, we shall only outline the essentials of the design process, applicable to any home publisher, whether he is buying out all his print, or proposing to print some, or all, or part of all, of his booklets himself. Design is the first process to be removed from the outside contractor and brought home.

Armed with a perfectly clear idea of what he wants, the publisher can then call for estimates from several printers. These may take time to arrive, especially if the job is complex. As we have seen above, considerable differences may emerge. Indeed, the highest estimate may be 100 per cent above the lowest. This may indicate that the printer does not really want the job. The cheapest needs to be analysed to see *why* it is the cheapest. The best plan is to get samples of work done, and to visit the printer personally and look at his premises. Anyone who has read this book will know what to look for.

The decision made, there must be a clear contract, specifying the details of the book along the lines shown on pp 58–61 above, and the dates on which proofs will be sent and returned — and final delivery of the goods.

When studying estimates, it is worth remembering that a printer often accepts work only part of which he means to do on his own premises. He may well contract out the origination of the text to a 'trade typesetter', the graphics to a blockmaker, the finishing processes to a bookbinder. All these make their profit *en route*.

Before the text is marked up for the printer, it must be copy-edited. It is much cheaper to correct spelling, style and so on when the MS is in typescript. This is part of the process of giving the printer 'perfect copy'. Books on copy-editing are numerous (see Bibliography). Briefly, even a small publisher must have a 'house style'. Consistency should be established in spelling (eg 'organisation' or 'organization' — both are correct), punctuation, paragraphing, use of double and single quotation marks, capitalisation (eg 'House of Commons' or 'house of commons') and so on. Even the smallest publisher must have a dictionary, and Fowler's *Dictionary of Modern English Usage* alongside it. The old textbooks on letterpress printing used to contain a chapter on that difficult art: hyphenation. The old craft compositors knew how to hyphenate. Photosetters, for all their computers, as yet do *not,* and modern typists or compositors often don't either.

Set in 10/12pt Century Roman u/lc justified across 27em measure.

~~HOME PUBLISHING AND PRINTING~~

(A)   ~~Chapter~~ 1 < 12pts#
PUBLISHING FOR PLEASURE

Chapter number and title
24pt Century condensed caps

36pts#

(B) 10/12pt u/lc bold centred

The Spare-time Publisher   < ½ l#

(Full out)

—— This book is about the craft of publishing books, booklets and periodicals in small editions from one's own backroom or backyard. It is a leisure pursuit or an occupation for retirement that is as suited to home operations as weaving, pottery, cabinet-making, metalwork or photography and comparable creative pastimes.

/set em indent

□ It can be done on a very small scale, or it can be as absorbing of time and love as gardening. It can be, or become, a sideline business, and make or lose money in the manner of other businesses. Its products can make a reputation for its practitioner, and it should lead to new experiences and friendships. It deals in self-expression and is itself a form of self-expression.

□ As in professional publishing, woman can and do excel in it. Irrespective of gender, it is something one can begin at twelve or at sixty - and continue beyond the eighties.

□ It is not in the least beyond the scope of people with disabilities; those who wish to do some of the production at home (see Chapter 5) can select the processes which can be adapted to their abilities.

□ Like other crafts or small businesses conducted in one's leisure time, publishing requires some outlay of money. How much or how little depends on the nature and scale of one's operations and ambition. It can be minimal: several of the

Fig 4 First page of a typical typescript marked up by the publisher's designer for the printer. See opening page of text of this book

After copy-editing, the edited copy is marked up for the printer. Every publisher should know how to mark up copy for the printer, even if he is his own printer. Otherwise he is bodging along and will waste time and money having second thoughts in the middle of the job. Pre-planning in this, as in every industrial process, is the secret of smooth and economic operation. Marking up includes the specifying of measure, type sizes etc, and is further dealt with in the chapter on design. Along with the marked-up, copy-edited copy, there should usually go to the printer a dummy or sketch of the design (the printer may himself offer a dummy of blank pages).

The stage comes when the proofs are delivered. It is advisable to know how to correct proofs properly, using a single system. We illustrate the principal signs (see Fig 5). If in doubt, any changes one requires can always be written clearly in the margin inside a box marked 'printer:'. However, for fullscale operations, there exists a British, and a European, standards specification to be had from HMSO. The author's perhaps amateurishly marked corrections should be transferred cor-

Delete character		Practice makkes perfect	Practice makes perfect
Insert character		Practice makes prfect	Practice makes perfect
Change character		Practie makes perfect	Practice makes perfect
Change to capitals		practice makes perfect	Practice makes perfect
Change to lower case		Practice makes Perfect	Practice makes perfect
Change to italic		Practice makes perfect	Practice *makes perfect*
Re-set in bold type		Practice makes perfect	**Practice** makes perfect
Re-set in small caps.		Practice makes perfect	PRACTICE makes perfect
Transpose		Practice perfect makes	Practice makes perfect
Reverse character		Practice umkes perfect	Practice makes perfect
Insert quotation marks		Practice makes perfect	'Practice makes perfect'
Insert punctuation stop		Practice makes perfect	Practice makes perfect.
Inset 1 em		Practice makes perfect	Practice makes perfect
Set out 1 em		Practice makes perfect	Practice makes perfect
Close up		Practice makes perfect	Practice makes perfect
Space out		Practicemakes perfect	Practice makes perfect
Insert word		Practic perfect	Practice makes perfect
Change word		Practice makes perfect	Practice renders perfect
Wrong fount		Practice makes perfect	Practice makes perfect

Fig 5 Some of the commonest symbols used in the correcting of proofs. It is always possible to clarify an instruction to the printer by adding a note in the margin thus 'PRINTER: ...'

rectly to the publisher's set of proofs. (Just because one may originate one's own manuscript, there is no reason for not proof-correcting it accurately, and every reason for getting a second pair of eyes on it.) A surprising number of literary or journalistic folk not only know nothing about printing but do not know how to correct proofs of their own writing. Some even despise such mechanics' work — and are self-righteous in their complaints if they find any errors in the finished work.

The proofs will come back with corrections in green from the printer's own proof readers — these are not to be charged for on the bill. It is now common practice to mark additional printer's errors in red, editorial mistakes (eg spelling, grammar) in blue, and the author's factual amendments or new inserts in black. The latter two are chargeable. Some learned books require a second or third set of proofs to be submitted for changes; this is unlikely to concern the home publisher.

Copyright

The question of copyright of course arises at the planning stage of any book. We mention it at the end of this chapter because it is a complex matter for professional publishers, but few home publishers will need to know more than the elements. His bookshelf should carry the law of copyright. This extends far beyond books and periodicals into art and performances of the arts; and modern technology has made it a controversial matter for legislation. The Museums Association published a handy Information Sheet on the subject (but see the Bibliography). We shall not attempt to summarise the law. Basically, copyright is a right of property. There is no copyright protection in ideas or facts; it is, to use the Museum Association's words, only the visual or verbal clothing of ideas or facts that is copyright. Any publisher or printer should know — as should any member of the public — that original text matter, illustrations, photographs, *and layouts* of particular books are protected by copyright for periods of years which are finite and laid down. Anyone reproducing old printed texts needs to be sure that these have gone beyond the limit and are in the 'public domain'.

There are also rules about the length of quotations from a copyright work which can be used without getting permission from the copyright-owner. We refer to this subject again in Chapter 10, p 161. It is so easy to 'strip in' a picture or cartoon clipped from the periodical press into a paste-up for offset-litho reproduction that its copyright status may be overlooked. We have innocently breached the rule ourselves and we know the vexation all round if the copyright-holder feels aggrieved.

Authors that the home publisher brings out and perhaps prints himself, hold the copyright, and he should indicate this in the colophon printed on the back of the title-page; and this is the case whether he pays the author or not. Many printer-publishers think the time, care and money they put into bringing out a minority work is recompense enough to the author.

Yet the most unlikely books suddenly acquire interest and become quite valuable properties. We think it is best for even minimal publishers and authors to make their position clear. An exchange of letters will do. Paying royalties on sales of small editions is usually an administrative nonsense. We have found that the simplest plan is to pay, by means of a nominal fee (say £5) and a stipulated number of free copies, for the 'first serial rights' of an original work. When the edition is exhausted, or after a stated period, the author is free to find another publisher or negotiate a new edition. Such a fee is legally a 'consideration'. Where the author is much indebted to the publisher for bringing him out at all, he often agrees to buy a number of copies. We never stipulate this. It smacks of vanity publishing. It's nice if the author does so voluntarily.

5
HOME PRODUCTION: THE CHOICES

Time and cost

The opposite pole to paying a commercial printer to produce a book from typescript to dustjacket is to originate, print and bind it entirely oneself. Many do. So far we have compared the out-of-pocket cost and the time involved, but not as yet considered the cost of the equipment needed at each stage of doing it yourself.

Each stage — because there are many gradations possible between having everything professionally done, and doing everything at home. The problem is to choose just that amount of home production which suits one's personal circumstances. To make the choice assumes one can acquire the appropriate skills. Some people can acquire none of them; but all the skills for simple book production are for most people readily acquired.

The estimates given on pages 59–60 provoke the question which of the four or five main elements in printers' bills could be cut by doing that process at home. They require differing amounts of time and equipment as well as personal aptitude. Some people prefer to do the earlier stages of design and origination. Others prefer to design and finish the book, buying from the printer only the printed sheets.

Just as the printer may subcontract parts of the book-making to subcontractors, so the home publisher can subcontract to local firms particular processes. In the past trade unionism would have made that difficult for amateurs. The new technologies and attitudes have changed all that.

When a book is printed commercially by letterpress, only the finishing stages can be done at home, but, as our estimates show, this may be 25–30 per cent of the cost. Otherwise it is necessary to buy a plant capable of all the other stages. In the production of a book by offset-litho, however, the home publisher can pick on almost any stage to do at home.

Let us begin, therefore, by setting out the various stages of the two main processes in tabular form. Bracketed items may or may not be involved:

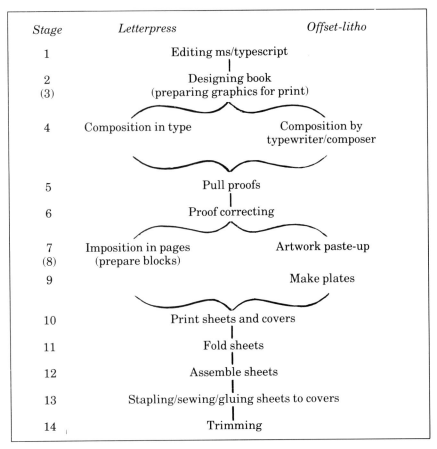

Stage	Letterpress	Offset-litho
1	Editing ms/typescript	
2 (3)	Designing book (preparing graphics for print)	
4	Composition in type	Composition by typewriter/composer
5	Pull proofs	
6	Proof correcting	
7 (8)	Imposition in pages (prepare blocks)	Artwork paste-up
9		Make plates
10	Print sheets and covers	
11	Fold sheets	
12	Assemble sheets	
13	Stapling/sewing/gluing sheets to covers	
14	Trimming	

Thus many stages are common to both processes. Moreover it is possible to do some stages by one process and others by another process to produce one book. The text may be composed by letterpress but printed by offset, while the covers are printed litho from plates but over-printed letterpress. It is common to print colour illustrations on the sheets by lithography but the text by letterpress from type in black.

The choice of equipment

For the home publisher deciding to do some of the production himself, it may seem that the first decision is between small offset and letterpress at stages 4, 7, 9 and 10. We have pointed out that a letterpress plant gives the capability to print the book completely: even so, it is possible to have the type set or partly set by a trade typesetter and hold very little type in case, if one prefers to pay for composition rather than sweat at it, and thus to economise on type purchases (or to permit the use of a variety of typefaces).

If, on the other hand, one elects to print by small offset it is unlikely that one will initially wish to buy all the equipment for the entire process, for this will involve buying a process camera to photograph the camera-ready artwork and a platemaker to convert the camera film into printing surfaces. Even so, one has to buy out the plates. Chapters 7 and 9 examine the capabilities of the two systems in terms of cost, speed and ease of operation.

Before the choices are made, or any equipment bought, certain preliminary questions should be asked, and perhaps answered in the light of Chapters 1–3. What is the long-term policy of the publisher? What are his circumstances? He puts in his personal time. That is uncosted. But there are two principal costs involved in buying and operating equipment — capital outlay and running costs. Here there are always choices to be made.

The reason is that capital costs and running costs interact. Sometimes an expensive piece of capital equipment may change running costs (and the publisher's own 'time' costs). But care is needed: the claims of 'savings' on which it is sold by the sales literature are usually based on saving employees' time at whatever the current rate of pay is — usually very high. This is irrelevant to a home publisher. Modern technology tends to require a large capital outlay and higher running costs, but does so to save operators' time (or to produce a higher standard of quality). Raising output from 3,000 to 10,000 copies per hour means a lot to the commercial printer but it means virtually nothing in terms of editions of 300, and relatively little in terms of small periodicals. Breakdowns and maintenance may be a minor cost to a commercial printer who has to pay the salary of an engineer anyway. But they may be a heavy cost in time *and* money to an over-ambitious purchaser operating it discontinuously in a shed.

Simpler equipment may be slow, but it may be reliable at slow speeds, and easier to repair when it malfunctions. Any particular process for a book — for example some pages to be printed in several colours — can be subcontracted to a commercial printer and assembled along with the home-produced pages. The choice is between the minimum one wants to pay to outside contractors, the time available for the use of slow-operating home equipment, and the quality of the finished product that the publisher aims at. Personal circumstances affect the choice of equipment. Some people have a knack for operating photographic or electrical equipment, and so find that relatively complicated machinery costs them less in time and repair or maintenance costs than it does other people — who therefore should prefer simpler equipment suited to their capabilities. Again, it matters to some people whether they can operate equipment, or adopt production methods, standing or sitting

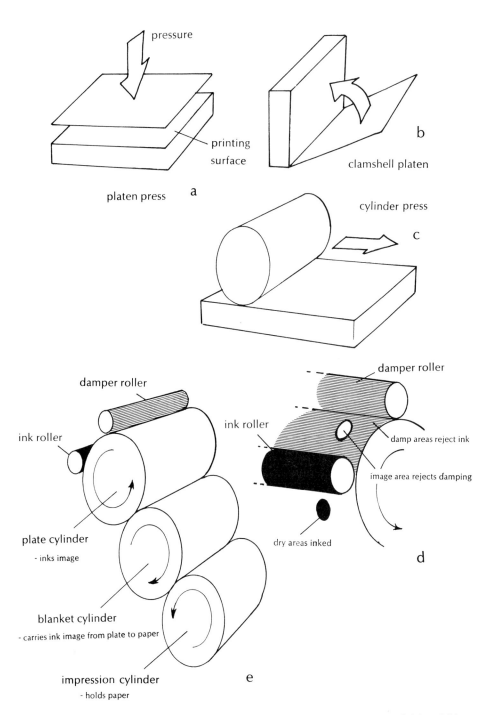

pressure

printing
surface

b

clamshell platen

platen press   a

cylinder press

c

damper roller

damper roller

ink roller

ink roller

damp areas reject ink

image area rejects damping

plate cylinder
- inks image

dry areas inked

d

blanket cylinder
- carries ink image from plate to paper

impression cylinder
- holds paper

e

Fig 6 Letterpress or offset lithography? A diagram of the processes compared: (a) and (b) the platen principle as used by most letterpress machines; (c) cylinder press as employed in proofing presses and large flatbed machines; (d) the litho principle — the methods by which it works and (e) the arrangement of the parts of a 'small offset' press

— one has to stand to operate a treadle-driven printing machine, obviously.

It is best to begin, after studying the options, and if possible going to see how others operate and with what, by considering how much one can 'afford' in time costs and money costs, bearing in mind that as one acquires skill, time costs are reduced.

At the risk of labouring the point, let us consider a publisher who wishes to originate pages of poetry for books to be reproduced by offset-litho. He can (a) set them in type by hand or by machine, (b) type them, either on an IBM composer or on a photosetter. Both alternatives give approximately the same quality of result. If he has more money than time, the last alternative is best. If he wishes to save running costs, the other methods are cheaper but require his time. Letterpress setting by machine or setting by an IBM composer will require substantial capital outlay, but only moderate time and little running cost, though more skill. Setting the copy by hand from typecases requires a lot of time, much less money, but some skill. A compromise is to hire, as one can, an IBM composer which would increase costs but remove the capital outlay.

A small diagram may serve to visualise the alternatives:

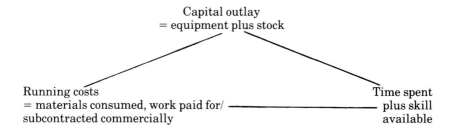

Capital outlay
= equipment plus stock

Running costs
= materials consumed, work paid for/
subcontracted commercially

Time spent
plus skill
available

Thus the 'cost' of doing something can be seen as lying on a triangle. It can be moved around, but to 'save' on one aspect is to 'lose' on another. Capital outlay saves time and reduces running costs; avoiding capital outlay involves putting in more time or using more materials, or dearer materials, and so on.

Finishing

The stage of production that offers the largest savings is in the finishing process — but, if taken home, involves a lot of time. Though this is the end process of book-making it is sensible to examine it first, because it is to the completed and finished product that all effort moves. It *must* look good.

73

In the past it has been common for private presses only to work at home up to the stage of printed sheets; these were sent out to binders, often craft binders. But in the past binding was cheap and short runs acceptable: this is no longer so, as we have seen.

For the simplest finishing done at home the only capital and tools required are an office stapling machine or needle and thread, and a boner and knife from the bookbinder's repertoire. This is enough for a periodical or simple pamphlet.

But it is not enough for a book which is to stand up to competition from professionally published paperback standards. Here, it is necessary to introduce the bookbinder's skill, if at an elementary level. First the sheets must be accurately folded using the boner to make crisp creases. Then the folded sheets must be assembled, fitted into each other in page number (folio number) order. Then they must be sewn. If a single section of up to 20 pages (5 sheets of four pages on each sheet) is the book, a simple figure-of-eight stitch tied on the inside gutter of the centre pages will serve.

If there are two or more sections the stitching is more elaborate and takes longer. The task is simplified if a template is made for prepunching the stitching holes (Fig 7).

The sections sewn together, the cover has to be fitted. Many little presses merely sew the pages to the covers, or, worse, staple them. It saves time, but will it make a booklet with bookshop appeal? We are strongly of the opinion that the proper course for the home publisher, who is doing his finishing at home and saving money, is to teach himself to fit a drawn-on cover creased to make a square spine: that is, a spine whose crease is not a V but a squared U.

It is simple enough, if a little time-consuming. The creasing can be

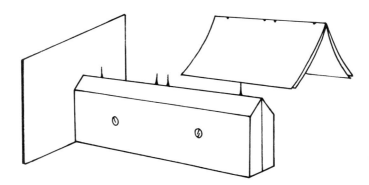

Fig 7 A simple jig for pre-stabbing holes for sewing booklets or sections of books made by trapping panel pins between two pieces of wood

74

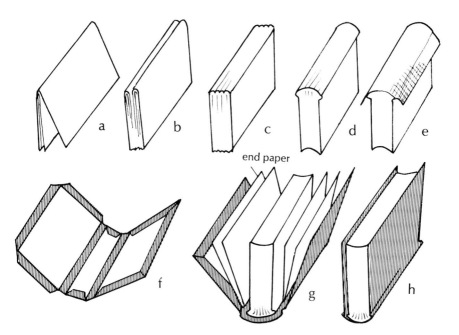

Fig 8 Sequence of stages in making a case-bound book: (a) single section; (b) two sections side by side; (c) sections sewn together; (d) rounded and backed; (e) spine glued and strengthened; (f) the case formed of card and cloth; (g) case being fitted to end-papers and book; (h) the finished book

done with a boner or blunt knife and a template made to guide the creases. A letterpress printing machine will crease a cover better and faster if the rollers are removed and the chase dressed (Chapter 9) with two lengths of brass rule separated by a six or eight point reglet. It is then also possible to print the title along the spine after creasing, provided the canons of accurate 'register' are followed.

The sewn section or sections of the booklet can then be glued (PVA is a sound choice) into the spine of the folded cover. Before the glue finally sets, the book should be placed between two smooth wooden boards, the spine protruding evenly about 2mm, and the boner rubbed up and down it a few times to give it an absolutely smooth square back (see Plate 11). The glue settles between the sections and the spine, and, if the book is of two or more sections, helps to hold the sections together. The book, or perhaps a dozen copies together of the book, should now be left under pressure for a day or two, as is always done when a hardback, or cased, book is made. Otherwise there is a danger of buckling owing to atmospheric changes.

Finally, the completed paperback must be trimmed. It may only be necessary to trim it at the fore-edge and top *or* bottom. But to leave it untrimmed is to derogate completely from the finished and crisp appearance it should have, even as a simple paperback. This involves one in the

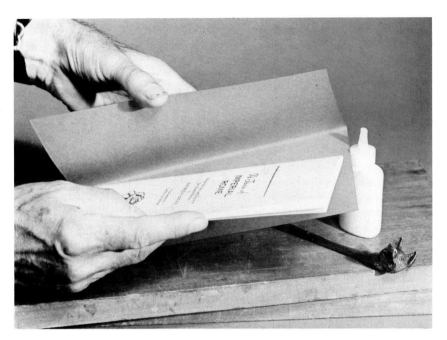

Plate 10 Simple paperback binding (1): fitting the sewn sheets into the pre-creased cover with a square spine inside to which PVA glue has been applied

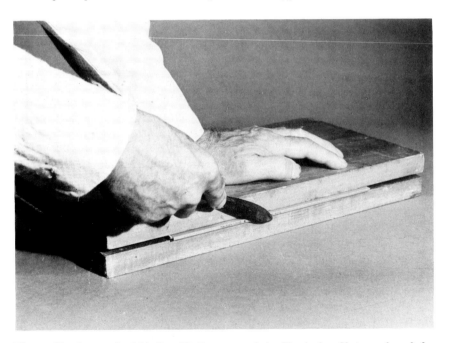

Plate 11 Simple paperback binding (2): the sewn and glued book placed between boards for spine to be rubbed smooth and flat with boner

76

Plate 12 Simple paperback binding (3): appearance of spine and cover after glued book has been trimmed

purchase of a guillotine or at least a sturdy card cutter. A card cutter, which will only trim one volume of up to 20 pages in a thinnish card cover at a time, is relatively cheap, and it is advisable to buy a new one, costing perhaps £50 (Fig 20, p 108). Anyhow, it is difficult to manage any home production at any stage without such an implement; for those who elect to make a start in home production at the finishing stages, it is the first unavoidable heavy item of capital expenditure.

A guillotine proper (Plate 20) is much more expensive, but will tackle almost any book-binding job, and permit one to accurately cut paper out of large sheets if needed. It is not necessary to buy a power-driven model, which can cost a thousand pounds and more, and is heavy. A lever-operated guillotine will serve most purposes, though it will be slower. However, the smallest model is now about £250 new. Second-hand models are not easy to find. While printing equipment, from typewriters to letterpress presses, becomes obsolescent and can be picked up second-hand fairly cheaply (see Chapters 7 and 9) the guillotine is an all-purpose tool needed in many processes other than book printing. They are also precision-built, and so retain their value in a lively market.

Nor is it cheap to obtain another invaluable tool of the bookbinder's craft — the nipping press or office screw press, which enables one to keep bound volumes under pressure at all stages of case-binding. The alternative is to stack one's books in even piles on a clean thick board, place another on top, and weights on top of that. This will not give the pressure of a nipping press, so the books must be left under the boards proportionately longer.

Perhaps because finishing an edition decently in this way does involve considerable time and care, many publishers opt for mere pamphlets. This would be fine if there were retail outlets specialising in pamphlets. But there are not. The alternative is to send the folded and assembled and collated sheets to a professional binder. As is shown on p 61 the commercial publisher expects to pay 30p per copy to bind an edition of 500. Few commercial binders will set up their machines for less than that. The home publisher, who will not be a regular customer, may expect to pay a little more than 30p unless he is lucky. He will not escape the chore of assembling the sheets as copies. The option is to save about £100, and perhaps some hassle, by doing the job oneself in the manner described above. An edition of 250 can be done in reasonable time. If done at home, it can, of course, be spread over a period; some home publishers, in fact, bind up copies as they are ordered.

How long does the process take? It is difficult to say. Our self-timing experiments suggest that for a one-section booklet of 250 copies, the folding of the sheets and the covers takes up to three hours. Pre-stabbing the assembled sheets takes up to two hours. Stitching, in experienced and usually female hands, takes 2 to 3 minutes per pre-stabbed booklet. Trimming by card cutter, book by book, takes another three hours (with a small guillotine, under one hour). If the cover is square-spined and 'drawn on' and glued to two or more sections before trimming, up to three hours extra must be allowed; and printing and creasing the covers may well be a slow task.

The alternative to stitching by hand (a modern stitching-machine is out of the question) is perfect binding, so-called. It is an easy and time-saving method largely used by professional publishers for paperbacks. The process can be carried out easily at home — but the possession of some kind of press or clamp and a guillotine are essential. After assembling the sheets, the book, or rather several copies (according to thickness) of the book are 'knocked up to the spine' and inserted between strawboards into the guillotine, which trims the spines flush. The assembly is then transferred to the press from which it protrude a few millimetres and is held down tight. The exposed newly-guillotined spines are then roughened with a file and to them is applied a coating of PVA. When this has dried hard, the assembly is removed, the books separated by a boner or blunt knife, and from the strawboards, and are glued into the square backed covers in the same way as for sewn sections. It is much less satisfactory to bind them into a merely creased cover (Figs 9, 10, 11).

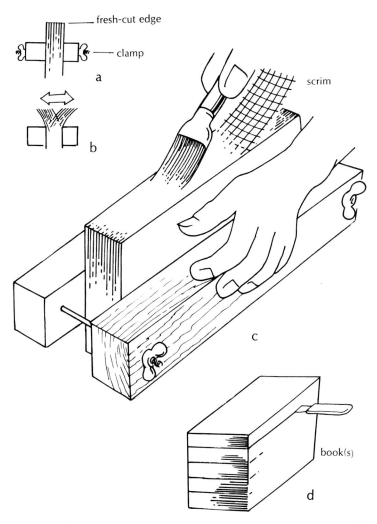

Fig 9 The 'perfect binding' process, showing: (a) book or books clamped spine upwards, with spines pre-trimmed and knocked level; (b) how spines are fanned sideways to allow glue to penetrate; (c) applying glue and (optional) scrim while fanning sideways with other hand; (d) separating a batch of booklets after drying

Variants of this method may be tried. One advantage of it is that single sheets, printed both sides, can be assembled and bound in this way, avoiding the objectionable alternative of stitching down the edges. It is also possible to insert single *folded* sheets, printed pages 1 to 4, 4 to 8, 9 to 12 and so on, without using a guillotine to cut off the spines flush. The folded 'fours' are simply inserted, knocked up smooth to their folds in the nipping press, and the PVA applied to them after a very slight roughening by the file; a better bond is secured and the book opens somewhat better.

79

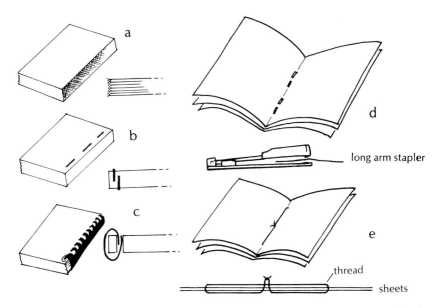

Fig 10 Some methods of binding slim volumes: (a) 'perfect' flexible glue binding; (b) side-stabbing with staples; (c) plastic or metal comb or spiral binding as used in special art books; (d) centre-stapled sheets, requiring a long-arm stapler; (e) sewing, showing a 'figure-of-eight' stitch

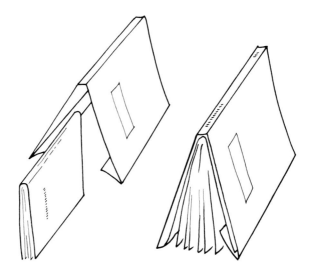

Fig 11 Fitting a wrapper to a booklet; note turned-in fore-edges

Perfect binding by PVA, however, is really only practicable for books of a minimum thickness of about 4 millimetres. If the method is adopted for binding 16-page pamphlets, a very thick paper had best be chosen. We make no apology for emphasising the importance of the finishing process for the home publisher, precisely because it is so closely allied to the whole issue of appearance and bookshelf appeal. We believe that the time put into producing a good-looking paperback by any of the above methods is immensely worth while, personally satisfying, and permits a net price which rewards the effort and gives the retail outlet a better financial incentive to stock it. The design and printing of eye-catching covers will be considered later.

The acquisition of these elementary bookbinding skills adequate to produce a good-looking paperback or paper-covered book are a useful introduction to the larger skills of bookbinding in the fullest sense. Those who wish to pursue this separate craft are advised to study the appropriate manuals such as *Bookbinding* by Eric Burdett (see Bibliography).

Even when the greater part of the edition is paperback, there is much to be said for a 'library edition' in hardback. If one has the skill to knock up a dozen cloth cases for a special edition to be signed by the author — and the artist, if illustrated — substantial prices can be charged, usually five or six times that of the ordinary edition. The profit on the special edition will inevitably be much less if one has the binding done by a craft bookbinder.

Origination and artwork

The other major saving in book production is to do the early stages entirely at home. These are design, composition of the text, and preparation of camera-ready copy for commercial machining of the sheets by offset-litho. The preparation of camera-ready copy, like the finishing stages, requires a minimum of capital equipment. The process is explained more fully in Chapter 7, as it logically follows the process of design. Here it may be initially said that, at its simplest, all it requires is a drawing-board, a T-square and set-square, a type-scale, and a blue pencil, plus such office items as adhesive tape and cow gum. Total cost will hardly be £25.

This is all that is required up to the printing stage if the intention is simply to reproduce existing out-of-copyright material, whether printed text or illustration or both. The same is true of original texts which the home (or professional) calligrapher can produce himself. Paste-up work can be done on the dining table, though it is more conducive to really good work to have a proper studio.

If camera-ready copy is made to professional standards the printer is left only with platemaking and printing and a highly professional book emerges.

The same can be said of preparing a book of photographs for plate-making and printing; but the reader is advised to note certain complications explained in Chapter 7.

Anyone who studies the process of 'paste-up' will probably conclude that it is well worth mastering. It is creative and itself immensely suggestive of new ways of presenting graphic design in books. The procedures are summarised in Chapter 7.

When doing one's own paste-ups it is possible to use material from all sorts of non-copyright sources — motifs and special effects which no commercial printer would be bothered with; and to make visual experiments which no professional publisher would risk. One is tempted to adapt Sir Winston Churchill on learning to paint: 'The drawing board cannot hit back!' It costs nothing (except time) to scrap a lay-out that is unsatisfactory and start afresh.

We cannot put a detailed time budget on paste-up work. It ought to take as much time as it ought to take. Time is not a consideration, except when making paste-ups for a periodical with a deadline. However, a routine paste-up of four pages of camera-ready copy for a standard book should not take much more than two to three hours, depending on whether it has illustration or ornamentation or not, and following an accurate design and 'dummy' of the book.

The preparation of camera-ready copy does not depend on doing one's own text-setting; this can, as we have said, be subcontracted to a trade-setter in various forms of typography, or, if typewriter origination will do, from a competent free-lance typist.

Text composition

However, it is obvious that large savings can also be made if one can produce one's own text and not buy it out. Typewriters are not a large capital item, and most people have them anyway. The majority of books and pamphlets from the little presses are produced by typewriters and offset-litho, as are almost all small periodicals. But whereas a little practice with the preparation of camera-ready copy will result in acceptable layouts for periodicals of A4 or A5 format, to achieve acceptable standards in book layouts with typewritten texts is far harder.

Typewriting is *not* an adequate substitute for typography. Its shortcomings are only somewhat less obvious when the text is poetry which has irregular line lengths. Long typewritten prose texts, with a 'ragged right-hand margin' are wearisome to read. Such texts are acceptable in

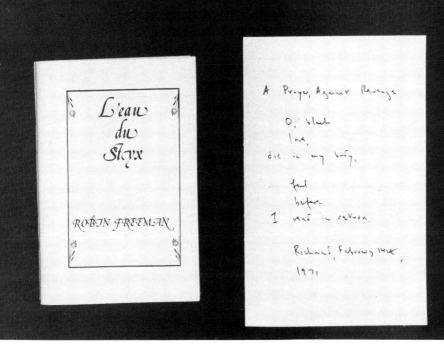

Plate 13 Offset-litho processes permit books with calligraphic texts or holographs to be printed cheaply and offer the alternative of the calligraphic title-page to conventional typography by dry transfer lettering. (*Top*) *Love Poems* by Augustus Young, calligraphy by Dennis Hadfield, from Advent Books; (*bottom left*) *L'eau du Styx* by Robin Freeman from Hunting Raven Press; (*bottom right*) *A Prayer against Revenge* by George MacBeth, from Sceptre Press

business or administrative documents. However, books are not a reading-chore handed out at a conference. They are offered as reading for pleasure. Typewritten, they are at the lower end of the scale in amateurishness. Moreover to be readable at all: (a) they must be originated on a typewriter fitted with a carbon ribbon which is more expensive than the ubiquitous home manual portable and (b) the publisher must arrange for his paste-up, margins and all, to be capable of a 15–25 per cent photographic reduction in size to minimise the ugliness and obvious non-typographic characteristics of typewriter type styles.

The use of calligraphy is superior to typewritten texts, and the only objection to calligraphic books is that we are so used to typographic books. Typefaces are descended from medieval calligraphic hands. It has often been remarked that if Gutenburg had invented lithography rather than printing with movable types, our books would now all be originated in hand-writing, and reproduced by offset-litho. In short, it is easy to like calligraphy for captions, titles, headings and some poetry, but not for long texts like fiction.

A carbon ribbon improves the evenness of a typewritten text, and so does an electric typewriter using a 'golf ball' or 'daisywheel' system of striking the type onto the paper through the ribbon more evenly. This variety of typewriter permits one to change from roman to a related italic face and dispense with unsightly underlining.

The 'proportional space' typewriter looks more 'typographic' because the letters vary in widths and the machine's action permits this: it also permits, by a system of re-typing a text, the achievement of a straight, or 'justified', right-hand margin like true printing. The same is true of an even more flexible machine, the 'Varityper', in which the spacing is not only proportional, but the machine carries two type founts on the strike-on mechanism, and it is possible not only to vary the typeface but the type size.

But the only rapid and easy way of achieving a typographic appearance to the page is to possess an IBM electronic composer, which combines all these possibilities.

The costs of doing origination oneself with this hierarchy of machines, however, ranges from £50 or so for a cloth-ribbon typewriter to £1,500 for a secondhand IBM composer. These options are examined in more detail in Chapter 7.

Here it may be sufficient to summarise the time taken to compose texts by these various methods (at home or commercially) and the approximate costs of doing so.

Composing method	Words per hour	Cost per 1,000 ens	Approx. capital cost (£'s)
Typewriter:			
Manual, cloth ribbon	900	–	50–100
Electric, 'golf ball', carbon ribbon	900	–	130–250
Proportional space machine	400*	–	200–250
Varityper	500*	–	500–1,000
IBM Composer	800	90p–£3.00	1,500–5,000
Linotype	800	£1.60–£3.00	†
Monotype	800	£3.50–£4.50	†
Photosetting	800	£3.50–£5.00**	1,500 upwards
Handsetting from case	100–129	–	††

*speed when justifying righthand margin; unjustified speed equivalent to electric typewriter. **But see page 129. †See page 141. ††See page 144.

Perhaps we are a little hard on the manual workhorse typewriter. In communication of ideas, it has done yeoman service since it was invented, nowhere more so than under régimes which forbid private citizens to operate any printing process, so that they are reduced to circulating banned thoughts in batches of up to five carbon copies; the method known as *samizdat*.

The printing option

The last stage which the home publisher can take home is the actual printing. This is not difficult if he is content with cutting stencils on one of the strike-on methods above for printing on a duplicator. Second-hand duplicators may be had for about £30 upwards, a good one costing around £100. The drawback is that duplicators require the use of duplicator paper, just as photocopiers require (though not for much longer) a special paper; duplicator paper is soft and heavy to absorb the ink and is often sold at an exaggerated price (one does better to buy it from a paper merchant in bulk). Using a long-carriage typewriter it is possible to type the stencil sideways to form a 'book' with pages of A5 size, or smaller if one trims the sheets.

The cost of purchasing a 'small offset' machine, its advantages and drawbacks are examined in Chapter 7. Here we may note that the equation of time and cost is more complicated. A greater degree of time and effort is needed to maintain these machines than their letterpress equivalents. On the other hand the owner of one, once he has mastered it, saves not only the printers' bills, but also the time wasted in going to and from the printer with artwork and corrections and to approve proofs. Prices in the second-hand market are falling as the new generation of photocopiers provides growing competition to small (and office) offset-litho (p 129).

The eclectic approach

We deal with the letterpress-printing option in Chapter 9. Here we may note the creative possibilities of using elements of both systems. The owner of a letterpress plant can use his type and press merely to make 'repro' pulls of pages to be pasted up and run off by offset-litho, thus economising on type. He can mix repros of type with typewriter-originated texts, pasting in italicised words for example. Such a mix makes sense, bartering time for money if the run is 2,000 instead of 250, and improving the appearance of the text pages, both of books and periodicals. Quite a small letterpress plant will suffice, perhaps costing £80 second-hand. Indeed a home-made proofing-press and some type will serve. It will also print domestic items, invoices, etc. It means learning and practising two techniques — but why not?

6
DESIGNING
SMALL EDITIONS

Learning how to design

We urge that designing should be the start of book-making, however simple, at home. The word 'designing' should intimidate nobody. Like everything else in the making of books it is not complicated or arcane, but well within the competence of any intelligent man or woman. Many books have been written to give instruction in the subject. They are largely directed at those who intend to design normal editions of commercially produced books and other publications ranging from 100 to 500 or more pages. This may seem relevant to the needs only of those with the entire resources of the printing industry to call upon. It is not so. They can be read with advantage by any publisher or book-lover, and they should be consulted by any creator of home-made books. They all emphasise the importance of taking trouble over the design of even the most ephemeral piece of printing.

We give a list of books on design and typography in the Bibliography. It is a constant surprise to us how many spare-time printers suppose it to be quite unnecessary to read even one of these books, let alone collect a small personal bookshelf of them.

Apart from such textbooks, the raw materials for learning about design lie all round us. They are on our bookshelves and our friends' bookshelves and in bookshops in the form of well-designed books crafted to the purpose for which they were written and printed. It is a perfectly simple matter to analyse every attractively designed book one comes across, measuring the margins, identifying the typeface, seeking the secret of its charm for oneself.

Next to a small shelf of books on design, one might add a small collection of 'the sort of books' one admires and on which one would be glad to model some of one's own. This collection can well include pamphlets as well as books, especially pamphlets and booklets which would be within one's own competence. When running a small publishing house, too, one can exchange with others doing the same, and learn both from what one approves and disapproves in their efforts.

87

Books about design inevitably carry only a limited number of reproductions of good designs; but good books are everywhere to examine critically, always with the thought 'Why do I like/dislike this? Could I have done it better?' And one can add the further question, 'Is this something anyone would think worth the price they're asking for it?'

From the beginning one is thinking of the audience, customer and market at which one is aiming — or rather casting a fly for.

From such a study one acquires naturally a sense of the conventions of professional publishing in terms of a book's appearance, typographical and stylistic arrangement, order of contents, use of paper and white space.

The end-result of a home publisher's work is, as we have said, mainly a fairly slim oblong or squarish paperback with a professional finish to both cover and layout of the contents. The difference between the professionally designed book and the home-made book, ideally, should only be in thickness. In every other possible way it should exploit the whole range of book layouts and techniques used by the professional publisher (and some private-press artists go beyond them). Most professionally produced books are of ten to twenty 'sections' of sixteen pages, whereas most home-produced books are of only one section of sixteen to twenty-four pages. However, many professionally-produced books are also quite slim, and these provide useful object-lessons. Of any one of them, the home publisher can ask, 'Could I produce this myself, could I do it more interestingly?'

From idea to bookshelf

Thus the composition of a book in type, or its origination in some other form, and getting it into proof — which is where most designers and print buyers begin — is to be seen as only one process in the sequence. The designer has to think of much more than the layout of type or graphics on a page: he should first think out the book as a whole from its subject-matter to the final finishing and presentation in covers (or jacketed cloth cases if this is called for).

The main independent variables in the design of a book are : (a) size of page; (b) size of printed area per page; (c) words per page in any given typeface and measure; (d) number of pages; (e) thickness of paper. To these may be added (f) use of colour; (g) decoration and the space given to it; (h) suitability of typeface to subject. Juggling with these in terms of manuscript and graphics, whether for a slim or a thick volume, constitutes the practice of book design.

Where to begin? Oddly enough, the first thing the designer might consider is the *spine* of his book. In support of our emphasis on the importance of square-backed paperback binding in the previous chapter, we may cite Ruari McLean, a leading designer, who points out that the spine is the most important facet of a book inasmuch as, on the bookshop or library shelf, it is the *first* part of a book that the reader or buyer sees. To take the trouble to form a proper spine is a waste of time unless the title and author are printed on it (usually from top to bottom lengthwise).

It is not easy to print on a thin spine of $1/8$ to $1/6$ inch (a pica em) thickness; nor is it easy to crease such a channel, except on a fairly thin card (180gsm); nor is the 'spine end view' of such a book terribly impressive. Even so, it should be done; if the text of the booklet is shortish, then from the first the designing of the book needs to be directed to 'bulking it' or 'driving out the matter' in the interest of providing a reasonably recognisable lettered spine.

This is no meretricious proposal. All publishers do exactly that when faced with a shorter manuscript than usual. (The days of wartime economy are unlamented.) They know that a book must look good to the public — value for money — a public that whistles at the price of a book if it exceeds that of a couple of drinks at the pub. So the home designer must think of using thickish, bulky and expensive paper (printing on fluff is no fun, especially for any artist involved), large type, smaller page sizes, the introduction of ornament and illustration. He can make a well-laid-out and illustrated short story take on the appearance of a short novel or novella if he so wishes. In any event, the first question to ask of a manuscript is, 'How much of a book will it make up to?'

Measurements

Before design can take shape, one must be familiar with paper sizes and weights from broadsheets to octavo (a broadsheet folded into eight pages). These points are dealt with fully in Chapter 11. Here it is only necessary to make some general points.

Sizes of paper, and the books made from these used to be expressed in inches, and still are in the United States. The metric system is now used throughout the printing trade, but not by very many amateurs, so we try in this book to give both.

However the basic module of design is neither inches nor millimetres, but the typographic point. There are to all intents and purposes seventy-two points to the inch (in precise terms to 0.996 of an inch; and one point is about 0.35mm). Thus there are six 12-point lines of type to the inch. This size of type used to be known as pica, and the pica em is a standard unit of typographic design measurement. An em is the square of the size, so called as it often accommodates the capital letter M. Six pica ems

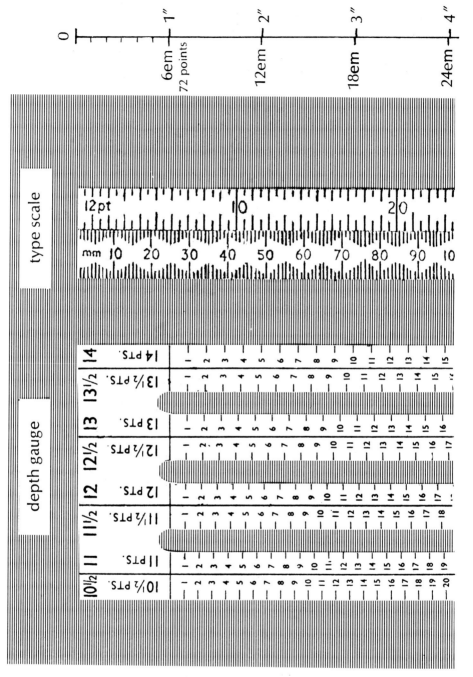

Fig 12 Typographic points and pica ems, metric and imperial measures compared, with depth gauge for measuring columns of text

90

equal one inch. Twelve-point type is a handy, readable book size, though ten or eleven point may be commoner, depending on the size and design of book. Anyhow it became usual to measure both the depth and the width of text in pica ems (and for shorthand reasons, in 'ems' — which always means pica, or 12 point, ems unless otherwise made clear). So a book with lines 3 inches long is said to have a 'measure' of 18 ems. The depth is also measured in pica ems. So if the text area is to be 5 inches deep, we call it 30 ems deep — whether or not the type size used is 12 point. A depth of 5 inches allows 30 lines in 12-point type — but 36 lines of 10 point, and 60 lines of 6-point type. Into this grid everything neatly fits, as a little measuring up of books with a typescale, graduated in points, inches and millimetres will soon show (Fig 12).

The coming of strike-on composers and electronic photocomposers or photosetters has not altered this arrangement; all can be reduced to typographic measures.

We have summarised the varieties of typewriters and their text-setting uses in the previous chapter. We must now relate these more closely to book design, since so many home publishers rely on type-written texts for speed, convenience and cheapness. Making type-written texts look tolerable calls for at least as much ingenuity in designing the book as do metal or photoset typography.

The typefaces of ordinary typewriters, whatever their mechanism, come in two main sizes, so-called 'pica' and 'elite'. (Some golf ball-type mechanisms permit a larger size.) What is called 'pica' allows ten characters or spaces, of equal size, to the inch, and is called 'ten pitch'. 'Elite' gives twelve characters or spaces to the inch. Thus the smaller typewriter size corresponds, roughly, to 12-point metal type size. The so-called typewriter 'pica' is about 14-point typographically — very large for most books. Both look even larger than they are because they are 'wide set', since an i has to occupy as much space as a capital W. Hence the importance of designing such a book for photographic reduction of the entire camera-ready artwork (margins and graphics to be corres-pondingly allowed for) by the platemaker, by one-sixth to one-quarter overall. (This improvement is not possible in reproduction by stencil.)

The need for this can be easily demonstrated. A commonly used measure (length of the lines) in book formats is 3½ inches — lines 21 picas long. This measure will accommodate 50–55 characters on average in a 12-point typographic type such as Bembo, Bell or Perpetua. But it will only accommodate 33 characters of a 12-strike elite type-writer type. The number of word-breaks at the ends of lines and ugly gaps in the texture of the text are correspondingly greater.

The proportional-space typewriter is an improvement. The letters fit better together, spaces between words can be varied in five steps, and

91

```
It is possible, if tiresome, to justify////
lines even with a fixed space typewriter.//
Lines are typed short of the right hand////
margin and strokes added to show how many//
extra spaces must be inserted on re-typing.
```

```
It   is   possible,  if   tiresome,  to   justify
lines  even  with   a   fixed  space  typewriter.
Lines  are  typed   short of  the   right   hand
margin and  strokes added   to show  how  many
extra  spaces  must  be  inserted  on  re-typing.
```

With five increments of space to increase   – 3 spaces
or decrease the spaces between words, it   – 4
is far easier to justify lines with a pro-   ...
portional space typewriter. The result   + 5
looks better. Copy must still be typed twice.   – 11

With five increments of space to increase
or decrease the spaces between words, it
is far easier to justify lines with a proportional space typewriter. The result
looks better. Copy must still be typed twice.

Fig 13 Justifying lines on an ordinary and on a proportional-space typewriter.
Note the marginal calculation for adding/subtracting spaces

QUEEN VICTORIA'S JOKE

QUEEN VICTORIA'S JOKE

QUEEN VICTORIA'S JOKE

Queen Victoria's Joke

QUEEN VICTORIA'S JOKE

Queen Victoria's Joke

QUEEN VICTORIA'S JOKE

Fig 14 Seven variant settings using a single typeface and size in Roman and italic

a ELITE 96 is another new
96-character type element. Selectric III
has a more powerful keyboard offering a
wider range of characters. Where maximum
utilisation of space is required use a
12 pitch style.

LIGHT ITALIC 96 is another new
96-character type element. Selectric III
has a more powerful keyboard offering a
wider range of characters. Where maximum
utilisation of space is required use a
12 pitch style.

This is typed on a "Daisy-wheel" machine using an
elite size face . The
wheels can be changed easily and some have both
roman and italic. This means texts with both can
be typed without changing wheels at all.

b This is ten point Press Roman *and its associated italic,* which is
the IBM Composer version of Times Roman. 123456789123456

This is ten point Century, a popular American bookface
and its associated italic, in the IBM version. 12345678

This is ten point Theme *and its associated italic,* a contemporary
bookface designed specially for the IBM Composer. 1234567891

c This is Bodoni Book (No. 600.8.C) set on a VariTyper machine.
Each type fount is in the form of a metal segment which, upon
depression of the key, is turned to the appropriate position and
then - unlike a typewriter - the paper pressed against it by a
hammer.

This is Bodoni Book Italic (No. 605.8.C) set on a VariTyper
machine. Each type fount is in the form of a metal segment

This is Bodoni Bold (No. 780.8.C) set on a VariTyper machine.

This is Bodoni Bold (No. 780.12.A) set on a VariTyper

This is Monastery (No. 840.12.B) set on a VariTyper

Fig 15 Examples of typefaces available on strike-on typewriters and composers: (a) Roman
and matching italic faces on 12-pitch (elite) 'golf ball' or 'daisywheel' mechanisms;
(b) three common book faces available on golf balls for the IBM electronic composer with
justified lines; (c) Varityper settings, showing different faces and sizes interchangeable on
the same striking mechanism

This is the design of Goudy old style *and its italic* in ten point set by photosetter. It is comparable with either Horley old style or Goudy old style in metal. 1 2 3 4 5 6 7 8 9 10 11 12 13 14 15 2

This is ten point Times Roman and *its associated Italic* in the version for photosetting. This is very close to the Monotype version. 1 2 3 4 5 6 7 8 9 10 11 12 13 14 15 16 17 18 19 20 21 22

This is ten point Souvenir Light *and its associated italic*, a style specially developed for photosetting with no equivalent among typefaces in metal. 1 2 3 4 5 6 7 8 9 10 11 12 13 14

This is ten point Plantin and *Plantin Italic*, a sturdy and popular typeface both in the version for photosetting and in Monotype.

This is ten point Trump-Medieval, and *its associated italic*, specially designed for photosetting but showing the strong influence of Bembo. 1 2 3 4 5 6 7 8 9 10 11 12 13 14 15 16 1

Fig 16 Five examples of book faces in common use for photocomposition and lithographic reproduction; compare with Fig 19

one can get 45–48 characters into a 3½-inch line (see Figs 13, 14, 15, 16).

'Strike-on' systems of typography only match the appearance of true typography when they are electronically controlled and the spacing and fitting of letters is far subtler; but such machines are virtually composers and rarely part of the home publisher's typewriter options.

Consequently, if he employs typewritten origination, he must design for them, using either an ugly page size (for a book) of at least A5 (210 x 148mm) or he must design for reduction by the process camera.

A further rigidity of typewriting is the spacing between lines. Type can be set (metal or photoset) with a variable amount of space between the lines by leading (see Chapter 9), but typewriters are fixed in their interlining and with a rather large space — 'pica' size is set to 18 point (¼ inch) allowed for each line, and this means that typewritten texts are very open compared with normal printed pages.

Margins

Whatever is decided about the method of text setting and origination, its location on the page is critically important.

Designers are traditionally more concerned with white than with black. It is this contrast which gives printing its readability. The white is so important that the designer normally begins after setting his page size by arranging the page's white areas, the margins. His or her aim is to place a grey patch (though type is printed black it looks grey as a mass because of the white between the lines and within the letters) in the appropriate place on the white oblong.

As most people know, there is a formula for doing this. The optical centre of an oblong is above its geometrical centre. So the top margin has to be less than the bottom margin. And since a book has to be seen as two facing pages — the so-called 'double-spread' — on the same principle the outer margins have to be wider than the inner margins. Any other arrangement, with a few exceptions, makes the text area seem to 'fall out of the page'. But what are the correct proportions? Here the pundits disagree. The conventional formula is in the margin ratio of back : head : fore-edge : bottom — 1½ : 2 : 3 : 4. Another is shown in Fig 17. That this looks about the best anyone with a sheet of white paper, a smaller oblong of grey paper, and a ruler can soon demonstrate to his own eye.

Conventions are not hard-and-fast rules. When publishers wish to cram a lot of matter into a limited number of pages they ignore them, narrowing the margins all round and adjusting the proportions.

The home publisher, with normally the opposite problem of driving

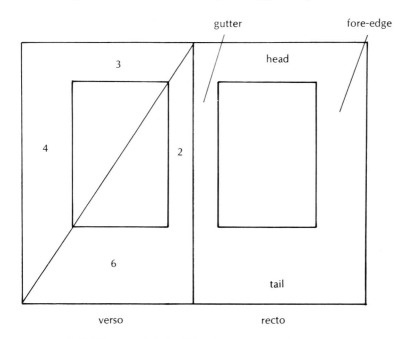

Fig 17 Diagram of the traditional proportions of page margins

95

out his text, will do well to think in terms of generous margins, as the great masters of early book design did.

Basically the function of margins is to accommodate the thumbs of readers, aesthetically to frame the text — and in former times to leave space for trimming after rebinding. All this can be achieved in various ways.

Texts are not always simple oblongs. This is obvious when one fits a text originated on a typewriter with a ragged right-hand margin, or poetry set in metal type. If the text is prose an average has to be struck as to where the margin is; and it generally looks better if close to a straight edge, such as the central margins or gutter. But this does not work on the right-hand page so well: some designers therefore prefer a narrow outside margin.

Paradise Lost has a shape like prose with a ragged right-hand margin as it is a continuous poem; but a book of lyric poems may have lines of very different lengths, stanza breaks and so on. Poets often see, and sometimes write, their poems as visual patterns. Only the eye can judge just where the poem is best placed on the page, and the eye improves with practice.

Again, an illustrated text poses margin problems. The illustrations may need to cut into or even be bled off (cut off at) the margin of the book. This is where the trouble taken to study design — to look at page layouts of books published down the centuries — pays off. The small edition must look good, and if illustration, ornament and colour (necessitating two runs through the press) are to the publisher's taste and he dedicates the time, he can settle down to produce books whose pages will stand out against the commercial product. And if the text has to be originated on a typewriter, there is an overwhelming case for using every other element of ornament or graphic counterpoint to improve and update its appearance; in a complex page design, it is even possible to make the reader think that a typewritten text was intended, not just second-best.

A glance at our illustrations may clarify these points. If, for example, footnotes are needed or quotations in verse, much can be done by varying the golf ball typefaces, or using two ordinary typewriters, one with a pica size typeface, the other with elite. Typewritten texts can also be 'lifted' by the use of printed typographic elements, like running titles set by letterpress, typographic borders and chapter headings or tailpieces (see also Chapters 5 and 10).

Specimen pages and dummy

Professional publishers often require their printers to set and proof specimen pages of a proposed book design — a double-spread set in the

96

type and proofed on the paper to be used. This is a good plan for the home printer if he has a letterpress plant.

However, the first procedure is to make a 'dummy' of the book; if it is a book of two or more sections, a single section will usually do. But if every page has complex diagrams and tabular matter, it may be necessary to design it page by page throughout. This inevitably happens when a paste-up is being made at home for offset-litho printing.

Nobody should set out to print even a pamphlet without making some sort of dummy, however informal.

The dummy consists of pages of the same paper (if possible) on which the book is to be printed (by whatever method) folded to the intended size, stapled (it is not necessary to sew it even if sewing is intended) and trimmed, and numbered as the folios (pages) will appear in the book.

The margins may well be worked out first on a separate sheet the size of the double-spread, but they will then be marked by pencil and ruler on page one of the dummy. A pin thrust right through the dummy at each corner of the printed area marks out the margins and text area on every other page, and the pinholes can be joined up. The cover should be designed with the dummy in front of one. (Is it to be trimmed flush with the inside pages as trimmed, for example, or to overlap by say 3mm, or ¼ inch, all round?)

It will now be possible to work out pretty accurately where the text will fall, page by page, taking into account any necessary graphics, and designing chapter headings, running heads, poem headings, initials, as work on the dummy best suggests, and the options and problems emerge. The number of words, and therefore the best lengths of line, will

Fig 18 Sketch of a dummy of a booklet, with a visual 'rough' of its title page

97

be known; at this stage, for example, it may emerge that it would be better to reduce/increase the number/length of lines per page, and/or alter the typeface size or leading (if this is an option). Indeed nothing is lost if the work on the dummy shows that a better book would emerge from a different page size, though it would entail a new dummy.

The importance of these calculations is enhanced if the book contains illustrations and other types of graphics, footnotes, and other textual interpolations or signposts that vary the format from a simple 'straight-setting' such as one sees in a novel. These may call for unconventional margins, or they may require the text to be set round them and therefore impose calculations of some intricacy where the lines will fall at top and bottom of the pages. Fig 18 and Plate 14 show a dummy and layout sketch for home-produced books.

The paste-up is not a substitute for a dummy. The dummy is a guide to precise and easy (and therefore clean) paste-up for offset-litho.

In dealing with a commercial printer a well-laid-out dummy, if only a single section of 16 pages, will help to ensure that the book he delivers is in accordance with one's intentions in the matter of margins and fitting the text and graphics to pages; at the very least he must have a double-page sketch.

If one does one's own printing, by offset or by letterpress, the same arguments apply.

Plate 14 A marked-up layout sheet by a professional designer with measurements in picas of margins and all type and space elements of the design (*Charles Maude*)

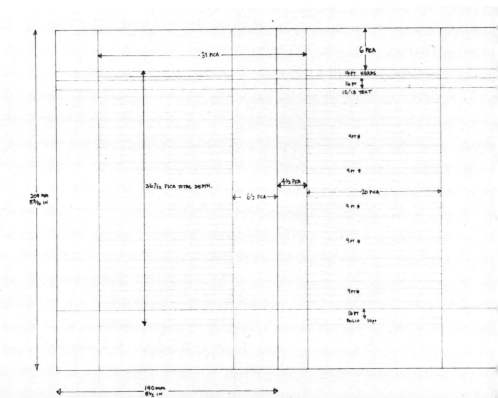

Order: the parts of a book

Many people read and use books without noticing the more or less standard order of their contents, and in this respect amateur books frequently show up badly. A 'slim volume' should begin and end exactly as if it were a professionally published book, even if such a presentation of its contents seems a trifle on the pretentious side. It is a good way of driving out a shortish text and making a book of it. It is fun to do.

Broadly the order of the contents of a book is as follows, though it can vary in some ways. Not every item in the 'prelims', as shown below, will feature in a home-produced book, or indeed any book. They are also given roman numerals, as is common in books, to distinguish them from text pages or because they are printed in a section separate from the sections of text; ordinary numerals will be better for 'slim volumes'.

page i	right-hand page or 'recto'	bastard (or half) title
page ii	left-hand page or 'verso'	author's previous books etc, or frontispiece, drawings etc
page iii	right-hand page	title page
page iv	left-hand page	imprint/colophon/copyright etc
page v	right-hand page	preface, foreword, introduction
page vi	left-hand page	end of preface etc, or dedication, errata, list of abbreviations, or blank
page vii	right-hand page	list of contents
page viii	left-hand page	blank
page ix	right-hand page	list of illustrations
page x	left-hand page	blank, or dedication, or acknowledgements
page 1	right-hand page	TEXT commences; it finishes on a recto or verso but
page n	right-hand page	appendices begin
page n + 2	right-hand page	notes to text if at end of book and not footnotes
page n + 4	right-hand page	glossary, index etc

These set out various possibilities; every book has its own particular set of prelims to the text. Moreover the preface or introduction may run to several pages; sometimes these items can be of considerable length in certain learned works. But these are the vital points. The bastard title *must* start the book on a right-hand page, whether or not a frontispiece is printed on the verso of it as the left-hand page facing the title page. The title page *must* be on a right-hand page. The list of contents, and the list of illustrations *must* start on a right-hand page. The introduction, preface, foreword *must* start on a right-hand page. The colophon, imprint etc *must* appear on the verso (a left-hand page) of the title page. If there are no items like acknowledgements or dedication to put on left-hand pages in the prelims, these *must* be left blank.

Let us now add a few notes on the features of the prelims, in the order set out above.

The bastard title (inaccurately but commonly called the half-title). Obviously this can be omitted in a small pamphlet. It can be used on the end papers if these are the same paper as the text paper. It is always worth inserting if there is a frontispiece or matter printed on the left-hand page facing the title page. It should be located at the top of the page.

The frontispiece Of course many books have none. If there is none, the title page looks better facing a blank white endpaper rather than the back of a coloured cover. If the author's previously published work can be printed on the page facing the title page, there being no frontispiece, that is a good advertisement for the book, the publisher and the author — he is not unknown to fame! If the frontispiece is a halftone photograph printed on a coated paper different from the text, an endpaper between it and the cover is essential.

The title page This is the most important preliminary page. It provides scope for design and layout. It should be designed, not thrown together with an odd line or two of a large type at hand, whether in case or in the form of dry transfer lettering. There is a small library of books on title pages and their design down the ages — every publisher should look through at least *one* (see Bibliography). Apart from illustrating a few amateur title pages in this book, we shall not expatiate. Those who are not 'into' typography will do well to look at the title pages of a few contemporary first-rate publishers and use these as models. Those for whom typography is 75 per cent of the fun of publishing will go their own sweet way, and good luck to them. Some title pages spread across the facing page — a frequent American variant to the usual rule.

Title pages cost a professional publisher money to have designed and set. Many therefore go for austere title pages which are inexpensive. The home publisher can well attempt a contrast and remember that in the eighteenth century a title page was often an advertisement for the

(opposite) ——————————————————————————————

Plate 15 Comparisons of title-page design in litho and in letterpress: *(from top left to right)* *Puffing Billy* by Richard Welford from Allenholme Press, letterpress; *A Pastoral Interlude* by C. M. Smith, from Laverock Press, letterpress; *Edgar and Emma* by Jane Austen, from the Kit-Cat Press, letterpress; *Moving House* by David Tipton, from Blind Lion Books, litho; *Industry and Genius,* anon, from F. E. Pardoe, letterpress; *Dick and Sal,* anon, from Shoestring Press, letterpress; *Topiary* by Alisdair Paterson, from Pig Press, litho

PUFFING BILLY
and its creator

1964
ALLENHOLME PRESS
WYLAM

A PASTORAL
INTERLUDE
IN THE LIFE OF
A JOURNEYMAN
PRINTER
1828-30

NEWNHAM
THE LAVEROCK PRESS

EDGAR
&
EMMA
by
Jane Austen

HUNTON BRIDGE
THE KIT-CAT PRESS
MCMLXVII

MOVING
HOUSE

david tipton

INDUSTRY and GENIUS:
OR, THE
ORIGIN of BIRMINGHAM.
A FABLE.
Attempted in the manner of SPENCER.
Inscribed to Mr. B ———

Re-printed from a copy of Aris's
Birmingham Gazette dated 21st January
1751

BIRMINGHAM
1980

DICK
AND SAL
AT
CANTERBURY
FAIR

An early 19th Century Poem
in the Kentish Dialect
of the period

HAND-PRINTED
ILLUSTRATED & PUBLISHED
BY BEN SANDS AT HIS
SHOESTRING PRESS
WHITSTABLE
1972

TOPIARY
ALASDAIR PATERSON

PIG PRESS DURHAM 1982

contents of the book. The modern publisher tends towards a simple title page and a lavish dust jacket to advertise the book's attractions. The home publisher, who cannot rival the commercially printed dust jacket (see p 104) may resort to his title page to even up the score!

We shall revert to title-page design in the chapters specifically on resources for offset-litho and letterpress.

The imprint Many private presses put their imprint, especially if it announces a limited and signed edition elegantly bound in leather etc, at the end of the text. For slim volumes this is acceptable if convenient. Normally it appears on the back of the title page and should contain the following information: (*a*) author's copyright and date; (*b*) publisher's name and address; (*c*) printer's name and address if different from the publisher; (*d*) ISBN number; (*e*) printing history — that is, a reference to previous editions or any such information. Some imprints are very elaborate and set out the terms of the Geneva Convention for protection of copyright and quotation from the text. If the book is to be sold in America it should carry a line 'Printed in Great Britain'.

Publicists who bring out pamphlets on Soapsuds in Industry, Imperialism in the Pitcairn Islands, the Alternative Vote, and so forth, in large editions printed commercially, often use the front of the coloured cover as the title page. Nobody designing books for pleasure will do this. A variant of the title page, especially if it incorporates a bold graphic, may be repeated on the cover as the cover design.

The other preliminaries in the list given above speak for themselves. It is common for home-produced books to incorporate one or more of them. All that need be said here is that they should follow the proper sequence and, above all, appear on the proper side of the sheet, right-hand or left-hand, recto or verso. An Introduction or List of Contents that appears on the back of the title page exposes the publisher's ignorance at once.

Type design

Many manuals on book design devote much space to the uses of, and differences between, typefaces. This is of relatively minor interest to those confined to typewriters for origination of text, and may somewhat bewilder those who decide to print their books and either to buy in photoset text from a commercial printer, or galleys set by a trade typesetter in metal, or, indeed have to chose what type to buy if they intend to set all or some of their texts by hand. It need not do so. The choices are, in fact, fairly limited and good taste and a moderate reading of a book on printing will pave the way.

Plate 16 Typographic type styles vary in size on the same 'body' in points, as shown here. In metal, this is measured by 'x-height'

This is ten point Bembo, which was originally designed in 1495 for the Italian printer, Aldus Manutius, and re-cut by Monotype Corporation : it is beautiful, *and very small on the body.*   1234567890

This is ten point Bell, designed in the late Eighteenth Century and an elegant alternative to *the perhaps better known Baskerville.* 1234

This is ten point Modern Extended, a version of the standard Nineteenth Century typeface, still used for *many learned texts.*

This is ten point Times, designed for newspaper use and truly of the Twentieth Century in its functionalism: large on the body and *narrow in set, to economise space.*   1234567890

This is ten point Perpetua type designed by Eric Gill, and a very suitable face for bookwork, & perhaps especially for poetry. It is small and light *and has a very elegant italic which is also called Felicity.*   1234567890

This is Gill Sanserif, also designed by Eric Gill, really a display typeface, suitable for captions and catalogues, &c., *but otherwise with only limited applications in book composition.*   1234567890

This is Horley ten point, an 'old-style' design of text face that is similar to Goudy Old Style and several others designed early this century. *The italic is plainer than really old designs.* 123456

Fig 19 Examples of seven book faces in common usage in metal

So far we have written only of type *size* and the space the various systems of origination occupy on the page. In the following chapters more is said about choice in typefaces, and examples are given. Those who have their books printed will be offered, probably, a choice of five or six well-known, but comely, 'book faces', as they are called to distinguish them from the 'display faces' used in advertising and display generally. Often a printer will urge a particular typeface because he has the 'mats up' — that is, this particular typeface ready prepared for setting on his composer, and can do odd bits of composition at odd times if his customers will mostly be content with the same typeface. If the customer is sick of Times Roman 10 point and demands something less workaday for elegaic poetry, his printer may have the book set by a firm that has larger resources — which means two sets of profit in the estimates.

What is a good typeface for a particular book is fully relevant to a chapter on design — but books have been written about it. We refer the reader who has the money to back his fancy to these. In fact a good designer will make an attractive book out of a limited choice between, eg, Times, Plantin, Baskerville, Bembo or Perpetua; the design, rather than the typeface, is decisive. There are typefaces — both those offered on golf balls for typewriter origination and those offered by printers in 'cold' or 'hot' metal — to avoid.

Colour and covers

One way to distinguish the hand-made book from the commercial book is to use a second colour throughout — but discreetly. For example initials, headpieces or other decorative devices can be printed in a colour contrasting with the text. This has usually to be a light colour not to be over-emphatic — light blue, terracotta or brown are effective; but initials can be in bright red. Such embellishments involve two sets of plates, two press runs and first-rate register — which calls for skill. It may be easier to achieve in letterpress, and printing manuals give precise instructions. For the publisher-printer with skill and plenty of time a distinguished book can result. It is important that the 'second colour' should harmonise with the cover colour and design.

Well-chosen covers also lend distinction. There is a very wide choice in cover board (in old parlance 'two or three sheet board' because they were built up in manufacture by pasting sheets together) but it has to be sought out; the local printer will offer pretty poor stuff usually. Good board in subtle colours and with engaging finishes is expensive, but shows up well in shops. The best way is to get samples ('swatches') from paper merchants. Book designers should be fussy about covers.

Bookshops prefer (and are now used to) plastic laminated covers or varnished covers because they suit a shiny consumer society; also customers' dirty fingerprints can be wiped off. However, lamination is an expensive process. Varnishing can be done at home in small editions. The cover design can be printed on a smooth white or tinted board, and when the ink is dry, each cover can be given a coat of clear varnish with an aerosol applicator. But they cannot be stacked until they are perfectly dry, and they have to be flattened under pressure. We do not recommend this.

A very similar effect can be achieved by printing the covers, or having them printed, on a kind of board that is very glossy on one side and matt white the other, known as 'cast coated', such as the Astralux brand. It will prove expensive, though not so expensive, and perhaps worth the cost, if one can print on it oneself.

An alternative approach is to print, or have printed, an attractive design for the cover in two or more colours on a white board that has a shiny side that looks laminated and a matt white side. The variety we have found satisfactory is known as Invercote D, and is not expensive. This option, however, is probably confined to those with printing equipment of their own. A 250gsm board for 300–350 covers measuring 210mm x 230mm was about £15 in 1983; the same in Astralux was about three times as much. Of course, everything depends on a striking and eye-catching design.

If catching the eye is not a desideratum, all that may be necessary is the printing of the author's name and book title on a good-quality coloured cover *paper*; or a cover may carry a printed label. Printed labels are easy to print at home on self-adhesive paper ranging from white to gold, if one has a press or if one knows a hobby-jobbing printer who will do it with care for a modest fee.

7
OFFSET-LITHO PRINTING

Camera-ready copy and artwork

We must now consider in more detail the options in the production at home of books by offset-litho processes, or 'small offset' as summarised in Chapter 5.

To prepare 'camera-ready copy' or 'artwork' for a pamphlet or a book is simpler than for commercial advertisements and periodicals which call for elaborate layouts with differing typefaces and complex illustrations or 'graphics'. This is the work for which textbooks on paste-up and layouts have been written; but they can be usefully consulted (see Bibliography). In layout and in doing the paste-up for a book, one is mainly dealing with identical oblongs of typed or printed matter; only on the title page are display lines needed. We have already discussed the question of design, margins, etc, in Chapter 6.

Although in principle book layouts and paste-ups are simple, accuracy is essential, for each page must replicate, in margins and appearance, every other page; while the verso of every page must 'back up', or register perfectly, with its recto, when sent for platemaking and printing.

Moreover the design may require the placing of irregular shapes within the oblong rectangles of the pages — there may be running heads to paste in, quotations or footnotes set in a smaller size of type; there may be drawings or photographs to accommodate, and perhaps tables or columns of numerals. The design may call for ornament, and the other possibilities described in Chapter 6. The layout of a particular book may at times be almost as complex as the layout of advertising copy, and a home-produced magazine will certainly call for eye-catching and varied layouts — considered in Chapter 10.

These points, however, explain why having the layout and paste-up done by the commercial printer is so expensive, because it is labour-

(*opposite*) ——————————————————————————
Plate 17 Paste-up requirements: (*from the top*) rotary paper trimmer, various papers, dry transfer lettering and adhesive tone sheets, adhesive and double-sided tapes, drawing-board accessories, pens for controlled line widths, typescales, fixative spray, T-square, set-square, and cutting implements

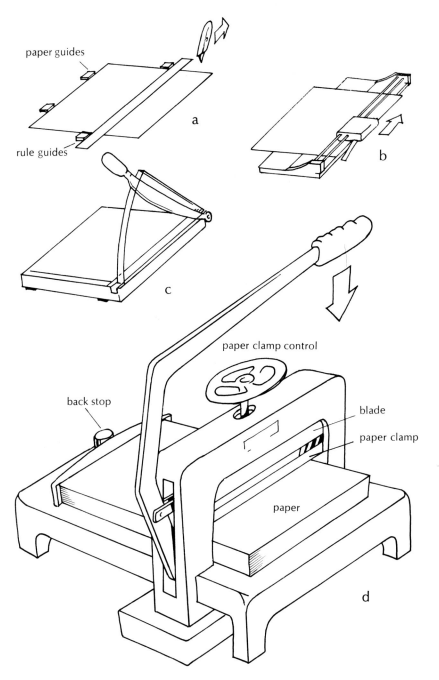

paper guides

rule guides

a

b

c

paper clamp control

back stop

blade

paper clamp

paper

d

Fig 20 Paper trimmers/cutters: (a) paper and card being trimmed with a steel rule and a sharp knife; (b) rotary trimmers for paper; (c) card-cutter suitable for trimming slim pamphlets/booklets; (d) hand guillotine capable of trimming a full-sized book (safety guard removed for clarity)

intensive; and therefore why it is so worthwhile doing it at home. Doing it at home simply requires an eye for precision, neatness and cleanliness in operation, and a readiness to take pains. On this depends the difference between a fully professional and an amateurish appearance.

The materials required are shown in Plate 17. These simply consist of a working surface — table or board about 2½ft by 3½ft, under a strong light; a T-square, a set-square or triangle; a printer's typescale calibrated in typographical picas and points, and in inches (or millimetres), a steel straightedge, long-fingered scissors or shears, knives, adhesive tape, cow-gum adhesive, and a blue pencil whose marks the camera cannot 'see'. A paper cutter is advisable, as already explained. Lastly there must be a supply of thick, very white paper or thin board on which the pages are marked out in the blue pencil. These comprise the studio.

The only expensive items are the paper cutter, and the lay-out board. Even the lay-out board can be a mere piece of plywood or blockboard *provided it is absolutely square*. For most people an artist's or draughtsman's drawing board serves best, and will cost from £10 to £30 depending on its attachments, such as, for example, a sliding bar that is absolutely parallel to the base for making horizontal lines on the paper and against which the square can be set to make the vertical lines.

The professional paste-up expert will use a 'lightbox' — that is a specially made drawing board that is transparent with a light underneath (Plate 18). These may cost up to £100, and are unnecessary for simple work, but, of course, a great help when laying out periodicals.

The first principle of camera-ready artwork is that the camera sees everything except white paper, white blobs on white paper (such as liquid correcting fluid) and pale-blue pencil lines. So not only will the camera exactly reproduce the pasted-down printed matter, but it also will slavishly reproduce dirty thumbprints, flecks of adhesive paste, shadows cast by any curling upwards of badly pasted-down copy, and any foreign bodies such as a squashed mosquito. The human eye-and-brain combination ignores what is not relevant, and even refuses to see what it does not want to see; the camera sees everything exactly as it is. So the paste-up expert trains himself to see his finished work exactly as the camera will see it — and has his eraser at the ready!

Unfortunately, anything that he misses and the camera records is irreversible, when it becomes the printing plate. Unlike letterpress the machine cannot be stopped to make corrections or adjustments. The platemaker can make only small improvements by touching up the film negative.

The second principle is absolute accuracy in squareness to margins. The nature of metal type requires everything to be square, and all that can go wrong is unequal 'leading' between lines — easily put right. Not

(*above*) *Plate 18* Working with T-square and set-square to design a lay-out with a light-box

(*right*) *Plate 19* Pasting up ready-printed pages for a four-page lay-out. The guide lines would be drawn in blue pencil invisible to the camera, and the operator would adjust each page with the T-square after pasting in position with dry adhesive such as Cow gum

so with paste-up. Every element in a page must be squared to margins exactly. This is easy when pasting-up pages of solid matter cut from galley proofs, for example (Plate 19). But when a page is made up of several elements, and when a correction has to be pasted over an error, great nicety of eye and fingers is needed. Any 'skew-whiff' will be instantly noted by the reader's eye as well as the camera's. By accuracy is meant square to a half-millimetre. Luckily, the human eye can be trained to such fine adjustments.

Plate 14 and Fig 21 show how two-page and four-page layouts are marked out on the sheet to the size set by the design and the dummy. Broadly, when planning a book to be printed commercially from one's own artwork, it is best to lay out as many pages as possible to reduce platemaking and machining costs. Normally this will involve a layout of four pages on an A3 sheet, giving a page of A5 size, or equivalent; this will mean two plates for an 8-page section, folded twice (at home). Printers charge little more for the use of the larger machine capable of such a layout. (Owners of their own offset-litho machines are unlikely to do more than print two pages at a time — see following sections.) Anyone planning to prepare artwork for a commercial printer is advised, for

economy's sake, to master four-page paste-ups from the start.

Let us now see how this will be done. Assuming an 8-page booklet is the intention, two pieces of layout board will be needed, one for pages 1, 4, 5, 8, and one for the versos, 2, 3, 6, 7. Each will be cut a little larger than the sheets to be printed. The board will be affixed by tape accurately square to the draughtsman's board, and then the outline of the sheet to be printed is marked out in blue pencil, with the aid of the T-square and typescale. At the corners L-shaped lines will be put in ordinary pencil to show the printer where the edge of the finished sheet is; these marks will appear on the plate but not on the sheet itself.

The rectangle so marked out is bisected twice, North and South, and East and West, by a dotted blue line representing the second and first folds in the sheet after printing to divide it into pages. Next, inner rectangles in blue are drawn in to the correct margins prescribed by the design and dummy of the book, so that, for example, the head margins of the four pages are 4 pica ems (ie 8 ems separate the first lines of each page), then the side margins are marked, at say 3 pica ems, and the outer, say 6 pica ems. If the matter is 35 picas deep (35 lines of 12-point type) the bottom margin will then be 9 picas (1½ inches). The lines can all be accurately connected up using the set-square. The procedure is repeated on the other sheet for the backing pages. The printer can then

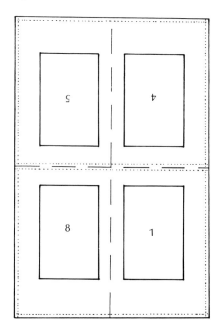 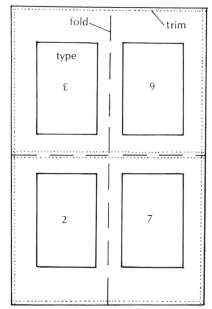

Fig 21 Two layout boards for a pair of litho plates to print back and front of a sheet which when folded is an eight-page section of a booklet

make the pages back each other perfectly.

The page numbers should now be marked in blue pencil: one sheet, 1 and 8 head to head with 4 and 5; the other sheet 2 and 7 head to head with 3 and 6. This is shown in Fig 21.

The printed matter, in the form of galleys or pages, will now be cut up with scissors to fit the blue rectangles in due page order according to the dummy layout. Plate 19 shows this being done.

The process of preparing camera-ready copy for platemaking and printing corresponds exactly to the (three dimensional) procedure of 'imposition' in letterpress printing. Plate 32 shows how in terms of metal type four chases will be arranged to achieve the same result as that shown in Fig 21. Fig 29 on p 153, the printed result of the 8-page section, will be the same after being printed letterpress or litho.

If the pages are more complex than those we illustrate, the position of the various elements can be marked within the blue rectangles before pasting them in. The matter is, in every case, arranged on the sheet to make sure that it fits properly, and is then pasted into position. The arrangement of all the elements in the paste-up should be carefully considered. There is everything to be said for a large enough work-table to permit both sheets to be spread out side by side. To paste-up several sheets and find that there has been a miscalculation so that a page is a line too short or too long, or other discrepancies have occurred, means peeling off bits of paper and re-pasting — a formula for messes that the camera will record.

If the booklet exceeds an 8-page section, care must be taken over the imposition of the inner sheet, which may be called B. Thus one side of sheet A carries pages 1, 16, 8, 9; and the other side pages 2, 15, 7, 10; sheet B carries on one side pages 3, 14, 6, 11; and its other side pages 4, 13, 5, 12. If the book exceeds 16 pages, it is usual to add a second section similarly arranged to carry pages 17 to 32.

When the paste-ups are completed they should be scrutinised for cleanness, and the elements rubbed firmly down with a burnisher (or spoon) and sprayed with a fixative so that nothing can come loose in handling and curl up. Even better than a fixative is a waxing machine (about £30) that serves this purpose and is worth investing in if a lot of paste-ups are to be undertaken.

A further point needs to be made. If the sheets, when printed, are to be folded and bound by the printer, he will trim them in his guillotine. This means he will reduce the top, side and bottom margins by one-eighth of an inch — more sometimes. If this is intended, allowance should be made when marking out the pages' rectangles and margins. These three margins should be appropriately increased, by adding $\frac{1}{4}$ inch to the gutter between the top margins and $\frac{1}{8}$ inch to the side and bottom

Plate 20 Power-guillotine trimming several booklets at once

margins. The longitudinal gutter, the fold between pages, is unaffected.

It is worth practising layout and paste-ups before actually pasting one up for the printer, and, though the system is basically just common sense, some people will derive advantage from one of the manuals on the full aspects of the 'art of paste-up' (see Bibliography).

Typewriting, origination and text-setting

The foregoing description of pasting-up camera-ready artwork assumed that the text was at hand. Indeed, it may have been cut from an old book to be reproduced by offset-litho. Or it may have been bought out from a commercial typesetter. This of course can be done, but it is not cheap; the costs, per thousand ens (150 words) have been shown in Chapter 5, p 85. Prices will change, and it is usually cheaper to buy in the provinces than in London. Broadly a page can be reckoned to cost £3.00 to £3.50 in setting costs alone (Chapter 4).

There is therefore a large saving to be made by doing the setting, and the entire origination of the camera-ready artwork, at home. We have explained the problems that typewritten texts set the designer (p 82), but if it is to be the chosen method, for financial reasons, there is much to be said for investing in a process camera (Chapter 10) so as to do one's own reductions to an appropriate size, as already explained.

114

But for a book to compete in the market the problems of the right-hand margin must be faced. Some people deny that it is a problem. Designers become passionate on the subject. Even so, the ragged right-hand margin is appropriate for a minority of books. The 'straight' ('justified') right-hand margin is traditional for almost all settings in prose. In Fig 13 on p 92 we show how this can be bodged with even a 12-pitch machine, and how it is more easily done with a proportional-space machine.

In essentials, it is the same logical procedure as that of the hand compositor justifying metal type in his composing stick (p 149). When the line is too long or too short for the measure (the width of the text in points or inches) one calculates how many units of space must be inserted between the words or subtracted from the spaces between the words, to make the total of letters and spaces 'fit' the measure. The compositor changes the metal spaces in his stick, having a variety to choose from and to combine; while the proportional-space-typewriter operator first types the line or lines up to or just beyond the correct right-hand margin, then calculates how many spaces he needs to add or to subtract between the words to make them fit, and then retypes accordingly, making use of the fact that he can move his carriage by one to five spaces along, rather than by only one in the case of the ordinary machine (see Fig 13).

The 'Varityper', mentioned in Chapter 5, is an alternative to the golf ball machine, but the later models (which are probably the only

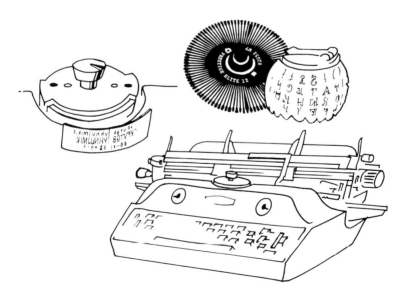

Fig 22 The Varityper composing machine and, above, a sketch of its unique typeplate used for changing faces and sizes, compared with the golf ball and daisywheel typehead mechanisms used in other typewriters/composers

ones worth buying) incorporate a mechanism for proportional-space typography. The Varityper uses curved plates with letters engraved on them which can be interchanged just like 'golf balls' or 'daisywheels', and a wide range not only of typefaces are available, but these come in four text sizes, from 6 to 12 point, and the mechanism can readily be adjusted to changes in size as well as style. Though these are not, like the IBM Executive proportional-space typefaces, true typefaces, they are much more acceptable than typewriter styles. The curved head carrying the characters, moreover, permits the mounting of a roman and its associated italic at the same time — like a Linotype or Monotype keyboard. In the later models, moreover, though the copy has to be typed twice to achieve justification of the line to the right-hand margin, the machine itself makes the calculation of what are the correct spaces to achieve this at the second typing, a great gain in speed of composition.

Is it worth substituting a Varityper for an ordinary typewriter the reader may ask. On page 61 we give the cost of originating a text of 50,000 words — something like £700. An IBM Executive will cost (second-hand) about £200 and a Varityper £600 or less. Obviously in originating such a lengthy text by either of these machines one more than recoups the outlay on the machine in the origination of a single text at home.

A better appearance will, of course, be achieved by setting the text on an IBM composer. This is still a strike-on mechanism with a 'golf ball' typehead, but it incorporates a computer which enables the machine to justify the lines to the measure automatically. The typeface is better than a typewriter typeface, and the speed of composition is at least equal to that of a Linotype machine. Such machines in 1983 cost about £5,000 new but were beginning to appear in the second-hand market at about £1,500. Clearly, the outlay on a second-hand machine is repaid after three of four texts of 50,000 words have been originated at home. However, maintenance of such machines is expensive and they must be serviced annually, like a car; and such a service costs rather more than a car service — up to £200. Even so, the excellence of the results obtained from the IBM composer is such that more and more small commercial publishers are installing them to originate their own books; and where they lead, the amateur is able to follow.

Obviously, if one originates one's text at home, to make the saving on composition costs, the preparation of camera-ready artwork incorporating it must also be done at home; few printers will do layouts and paste-ups of copy which they have not set and charged for themselves. (*Note:* 'Origination' in ordinary printing parlance means both the composition of the text (by whatever process) and the making of camera-ready copy from the composed text, together with the addition of illustrations, etc.)

116

Other firms make strike-on composers, as well as IBM, such as Olivetti, and some are cheaper; it is worth while studying in second-hand typewriter shops and the pages of *Exchange and Mart* what is available at any given time.

The appearance of a page of strike-on typography is now very good. Fully typographical composition can however only be achieved with offset-litho by installing a photosetting, fully computerised, composer and processor. This combination turns out texts in galley form, or even fully imposed as camera-ready copy, photographically reproduced without ink or ribbons. The type founts are held on tape and now have virtually the gamut of the old typefounders' catalogues, as required by the advertising industry. This is not the book in which to describe the amazing versatility of these machines, which have little relevance to home publishing.

The day will come when some home publishers, of books or periodicals, will be able to install a simple model. Second-hand, these are appearing on the market for £2,500–£3,000, sometimes less. As home computers become ever more familiar, the ability of the ordinary citizen to cope with these machines will grow. But the cost of buying and maintaining them will probably restrict them to those publishing for a living.

The cost comparisons for buying machines for composition are given in Chapter 5. The longer the texts to be originated, the better the cost comparisons for more sophisticated machines. Once one has mastered the techniques of small offset with short texts, it may prove best to hire one or other of the more sophisticated machines with which to originate a long text.

The publisher who composes his texts by typewriter or composer, and prepares his own camera-ready copy, will naturally turn to dry transfer lettering to provide the display lines for his title pages, possibly also his chapter headings, and certainly the lettering for his covers or jackets.

This technique is now so well known that it is unnecessary for us to offer any instructions. The finer points in using it are dealt with in manuals on paste-up. It has proved the answer to eye-catching posters for local jumble sales and entertainments.

The danger lies in its very simplicity and the very wide range of type styles that are now available in art supply shops. What is fine on posters often looks awful on title pages, and even on book covers. Moreover buying a wide range of sheets, or founts, of this lettering is expensive. The best plan is to buy only a little in styles that match, as closely as possible, the text typeface. An over-elaborate title page assembled from dry transfer lettering followed by a typewritten text kills both. Anyone using the resources of dry transfer lettering is well advised to study some of the textbooks on book design and typography.

117

Printing by offset

To proceed to add a printing facility to the capacity to prepare camera-ready copy and originate texts at home, it is necessary to understand lithography. The usual explanation is that oil and water repel one another and this is the principle of this process. True enough: but of surprisingly little help when one decides to print at home by this process.

To print by 'small offset' (a term we will enlarge on later) two elements are required: a suitable machine and an offset printing plate. The machines available vary in age, size, reliability, speed and accuracy of production, and ease of use; but will all perform the same functions. They will feed in the sheets of paper (unlike letterpress, hand-feeding is rare), ink the printing surface, make the print, and deliver the printed sheet. Because the printing surface is a thin sheet, it can be wrapped round a drum, and therefore the machine prints faster than a similar-sized letterpress machine — from 3,000 to 10,000 copies an hour. However, it is not so much the machine that has generated the boom in small offset as the offset printing plate itself, for there is a wide range of methods for making them.

The first question is whether one will make the plates for oneself, or have them made by the many firms who specialise in this — they are listed in the 'Yellow Pages'. The machine comes first, for it is not usual to make the plates and get someone else to print them. To have plates made, it is necessary to inform the platemaker of the size and model of the press to which they are to be attached, as well as to provide him with the camera-ready artwork, and to tell him what sort of run is intended. This point is significant because of the different kinds of plates made. Those that last for more copies cost more; for runs of a few hundred copies very cheap plates can be made. For those who decide to have their plates made for them, it is worth while to study the different kinds, and how they are made, to buy the most suitable.

Plates can be divided into three categories, regardless of the process of manufacture: paper, plastic, and metal. Their durability is in that order and so is their cost. The basic plates cost only a penny or two for paper, ten or twenty times as much for metal; of course the cost of making them is another matter. Durability depends on the run and on any mishandling. The beginner at offset-litho is advised to start with expertly made metal plates until completely confident at operating his printing machine, and then to move to cheaper plates as appropriate. Operating errors will not then damage the plate and one source of problems — faulty plates — can be eliminated. Litho can be confusing when things go wrong: a maladjusted machine, a poor ink, paper or plate, an error in operating, and results are poor without obvious cause. Our advice is to begin with as many factors guaranteed correct as possible, and to adjust one thing at a time to avoid risks of confusion.

Given, then, the choice of material for the plate, there is still the method of making the plate ready for printing to be chosen. Normally one buys plates specially prepared to suit the process intended, and these are readily available along with other materials from lithographic printers' suppliers.

Direct image plates are the simplest in principle, the cheapest to produce but have their drawbacks. They are prepared by writing, typing, drawing or printing directly on them with any substance that will leave a permanently oil-receptive surface. Special ball-point pencils, crayons, inks and typewriter ribbons are best used (though one can experiment). Great care is needed not to smudge the images or to get greasy marks on the plate by accident (eg from typewriter paper rollers). Those who also possess letterpress machines can print directly onto the plate. The combination of a well-operated Varityper or composer and skilfully handled direct image plate is the key to printing long texts inexpensively on one's own small offset machine. A layout is vital, but paste-up is obviated. 'Non-reproducing pencils' permit lay-outs to be marked on the plate for guidance in typing without appearing when printed.

After drying the plate will probably have to be wiped with a special chemical to 'de-sensitise' it, and it is then ready for printing, and should be stored with great care until affixed to the machine.

Such plates cannot print much more than 500 copies, depending on skill in preparation and handling. If one is damaged a new one must be made. But their advantage to the small-editions publisher is self-evident.

Chemical transfer plates ('CT plates') need at least a small exposure and developer unit (Plate 21), which might cost £50–£100 second-hand, and occupy two or three square feet of the workspace. To make a plate, a special negative paper is first placed with the artwork in the exposure unit, and exposed for a minute or two — the negative is not very sensitive, and so no darkroom is needed — and then the negative is fed with the printing plate between rollers in a trough of developer and left for another minute or so. When negative and plate are separated, the plate will have the required image on it which is 'fixed' with chemical wiped over it before printing. Allowing for chemicals, such plates work out at about 50p to £1.00 to produce, and take only 5–10 minutes each. But the chemicals have a limited life and poor plates result from using exhausted chemicals; so it is necessary either to buy chemicals every

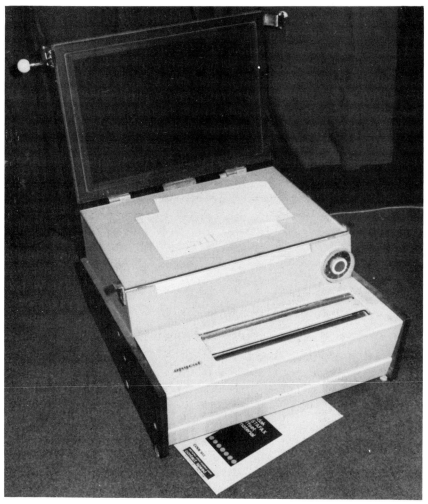

Plate 21 A C.T. platemaker with vacuum back at the top, glass plate covering lights, with exposure time at right. The front section shows slots to feed plate into developer

time plates are made, which is uneconomic since the plates are sold in packs of fifty, or so to arrange the run of artwork that fifty plates are made at the same time — enough for a 100-page book.

Electro-static plates are made exactly like ordinary paper electro-static copies used for photocopiers, but on specially prepared plates to fit the offset machine and survive the printing process. They can be made on any electro-static copier that can handle the size and rigidity of the plates: suitable second-hand machines cost £100 to £200. This process has been much improved lately and the newest machines produce excellent results with none of the loss of blackness in solid areas that the earlier models produced. When considering the purchase of a second-hand machine, the plates or copies produced by it should be studied to see how areas of blackness have come out. If heavy solids are not needed in the printing to be undertaken, the old machines can be adequate. Electro-static plates cost only a few pence to make.

Both chemical-transfer and electro-static plates can often be criticised for lack of sharpness, and so are not really suited to producing photographs, though sometimes they are so employed.

Pre-sensitised or negative/positive plates are the last major option. These deliver the best quality, the most flexibility in adjustment, and best control over results. Unlike the previous types, they require a process camera, which costs £200–£400 second-hand and takes up at least three square feet of workspace, and also an exposure unit (£20–£40). The original artwork which we have earlier described is photographed in the camera onto a special film known as 'lith' film, which reproduces the image in black and white only, with no shades of grey (see the explanation of line and tone, page 163). The film is normally the same size as the plate, hence the size of the camera. Because precise results are required, the camera has a glass plate to hold the artwork perfectly flat, lights to

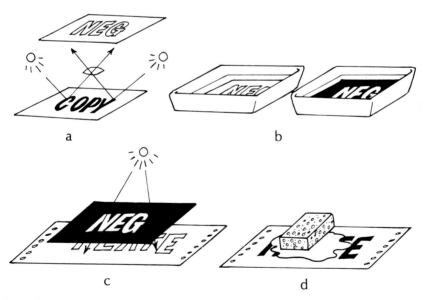

Fig 23 Stages in making a positive-negative litho plate: (a) exposing the negative in the process camera; (b) developing the negative in darkroom; (c) exposing plate using UV light in vacuum unit to hold negative firm; (d) developing plate

121

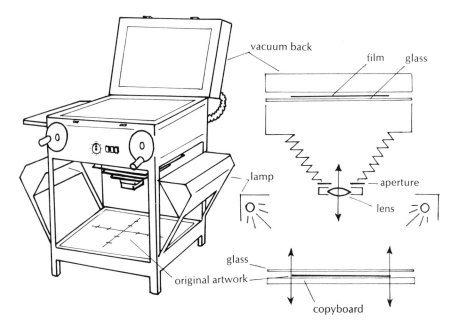

Fig 24 A small vertical process camera and diagram of its operation: the lens moves to alter magnification, and the copy board moves to alter focus

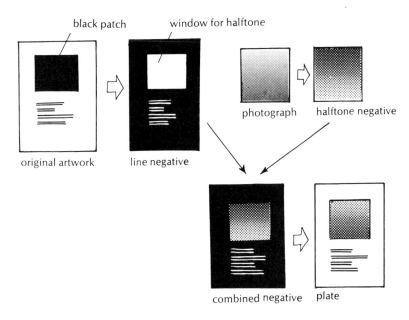

Fig 25 Stripping in: a half-tone in a litho (or letterpress) plate is photographed separately and then either exposed onto the plate, also separately or, more often, 'stripped in' to the main (line) negative to make a composite master; a black patch on the original is used to create the necessary 'window' in the 'line' negative

illuminate it evenly, and a suction-back appliance to hold the film absolutely flat and in position. The camera allows the operator to reduce or enlarge the artwork, which improves both typewriting and drawings.

If a photograph is to be reproduced, it will be re-photographed separately using a 'screen' to produce a negative consisting again of black and white only but made up of dots of various sizes to give a visual illusion of shades of grey — corresponding to a letterpress half-tone (p 167). This negative can be patched into the master negative where required.

The whole negative can now be re-touched to remove any blemishes as noted above: an opaque paint is used to paint over unwanted marks (which come out as clear spots on the negative). The negative is placed on the pre-sensitised printing plate, exposed to ultra-violet light, and the plate developed by wiping with the appropriate chemical. Such plates will print thousands of copies. They cost more to make because of the use of lith film and chemicals — about £2 for the negative, plus 50p for the plate. The negative can be stored for re-use.

This summary is not meant to be an instruction for making such plates; if this is undertaken, the manufacturers' instruction booklets must be followed; specialist books (see Bibliography) go into fuller details, though usually only on the pre-sensitised process.

Small offset printing machines

It is naturally difficult to describe in detail how to operate printing machines which differ in design, name their controls differently, and in varying degree differ even in how their operations take place. Two basic pieces of advice must therefore preface this short account. A buyer of a second-hand machine should obtain the instruction book for that machine and find someone familiar with it to run off a job, every stage of which can be jotted down in a notebook as it occurs.

A small offset machine, while operating on fairly simple principles, is a sophisticated and complex piece of equipment, made to high standards of accuracy; it can be compared to a car. Few car owners open the bonnet of a new car and adjust the parts inside without being sure what they are doing. The litho machine should be treated with the same caution: the rule is, only adjust when you know what to adjust and why. Each step should be mastered in turn (see Plate 23).

The machines typically print a sheet up to 10 x 15 inches in size, hence the 'small' in 'small offset', because, before their introduction, litho machines only printed full sheets four times that size. Many inter-mediate capacities are now available.

Upon installation, the machine must stand firm and level; if the

123

Plate 22 A modern commercial table-top small offset printing machine (*Roneo-Alcatel*)

machine is not precisely level the water in the 'fount' may lie unevenly and cause uneven damping and printing. Next, the machine should be test-operated without any ink or printing plate; the paper should just be fed through, to check the feeding and delivery mechanism. Different sizes and thicknesses of paper should be tried, to see how the mechanism handles them. Common causes of trouble are badly-cut paper, wavy paper (caused by bad storage — see Chapter 11) and, in machines which are friction-fed, a cause of trouble is wear of the rubber on the pusher-bar that detaches the top sheet from the pile.

Near the feeding point of the machine, there will normally be found two main controls: a lever to drop the paper platform and a knob to wind it up until the top of the paper pile is in position. The stack of paper should have guides to hold it in place. Most machines will not work without a minimum pile of paper — about an inch or so. At the delivery end, there should be guides to feed the paper through properly and to make it form a neat stack. In between, there will be an adjustment device, probably near the front edge of the paper stack, to adjust the squareness of the paper as it is fed in.

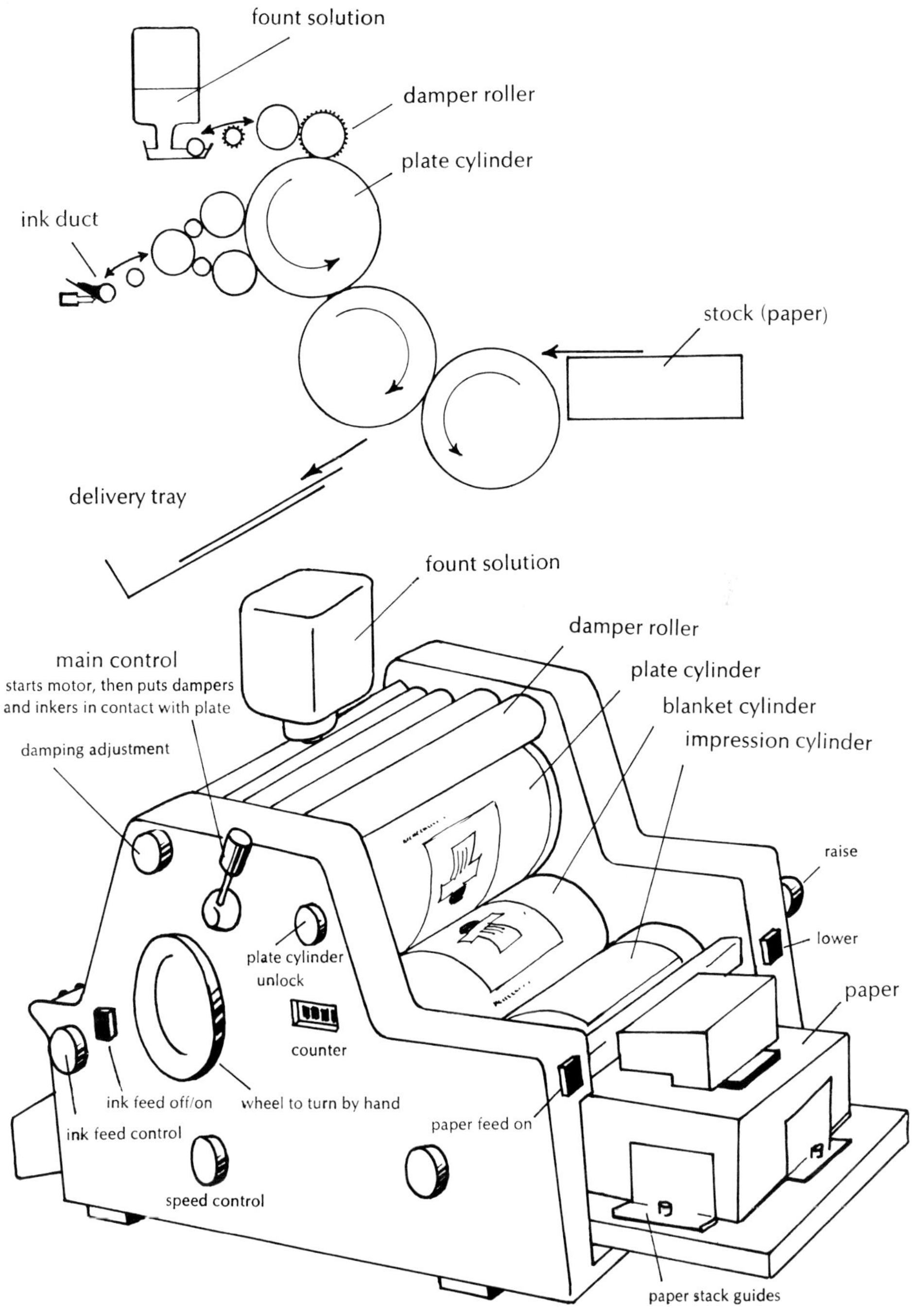

Labels in diagram:

fount solution

damper roller

plate cylinder

ink duct

stock (paper)

delivery tray

fount solution

damper roller

main control
starts motor, then puts dampers
and inkers in contact with plate

plate cylinder

blanket cylinder

impression cylinder

damping adjustment

raise

plate cylinder
unlock

lower

paper

counter

ink feed off/on   wheel to turn by hand

ink feed control

paper feed on

speed control

paper stack guides

Fig 26 Diagram of controls indicated on a typical small offset machine

125

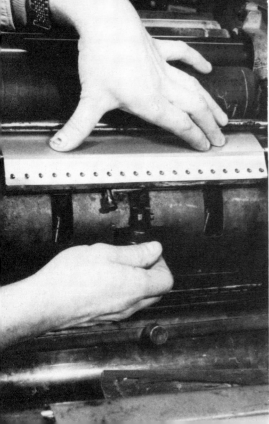

To operate the machine to feed paper, it may be possible to turn the mechanism by hand by a knob on the end of the main cylinder: this should be done initially to make sure nothing is 'catching', then the power can be switched on and the machine should now operate automatically, adjusting the paper supply as it is used up.

Next, the fount solution specified must be made up and placed in the indicated container, usually a plastic bottle at the top of the machine. The machine should be run to check that the solution is damping the correct sequence of rollers — usually cloth-covered ones; if the machine is dry, it needs time to absorb the solution thoroughly. It may incorporate a lever to switch the distribution of solution on and off, and almost certainly it will have a control to adjust the flow through the system (usually this is achieved by a knob controlling a ratchet that sets the degree to which one of the rollers revolves).

Two main systems of damping are in use. In the more common, the fount solution is carried by cloth-covered and metal rollers directly to the printing plate. It is used to wet the plate before the inking rollers run over it to ink the image areas: the image areas are greasy and have rejected the fount solution (mainly water) and so accept the ink. The blank areas, not being greasy, have accepted the fount solution and are wet and so reject ink.

In the other system the fount solution is fed by metal rollers to the ink rollers. At first sight this seems unlikely to work — but it does. However, experience has shown us that it is a little more difficult for beginners to master.

Ink is now put in the ink duct (a triangular tray at the rear of the machine). It is fitted with a flexible blade and adjusting screws so that the amount of ink fed through can be adjusted at each point across the machine. A second adjustment will allow the turning of the ink-feeding roller to be set, controlling the total amount of ink fed at each printing. These two controls allow the inking to be precisely set to match the needs of the job. The machine should be run to spread the ink over the rollers, making sure that it is evenly but thinly spread over all of them.

The plate is now fitted to the machine, usually by clamping bars or a set of teeth at each end of the cylinder. An adjustment loosens the

(*opposite*) ————————————————————————————

Plate 23 Setting up a small offset machine: (*a*) lever to lower paper-feed tray to stack paper with, left, the weight to hold down paper and right, the friction feeder; (*b*) the ink duct being adjusted: centre is a double knob to adjust total ink feed at each revolution and to feed ink by hand, right shows an on–off control which in steps puts machine into motion, dampers on to plate, and then the ink roller on to ink; (*c*) fitting plate to clamps and tightening, with cloth roller visible at back; (*d*) moving the printing position by adjusting the plate cylinder relative to blanket — the knob allows the plate cylinder to be unlocked and the machine turned left by hand to move the others as needed before re-locking

system to insert the plate, then tensions it: it should be firm to avoid damage or blurred images. Visual alignment now allows the inking to be adjusted more closely, as bold parts of the plate can be aligned with duct controls and allowed more ink, and blank parts none. This refined controlling can only be done when paper is being printed and the results seen. Presetting however saves time and mess. Depending on the manufacturer's instructions, the plate may need to be wiped with chemical or water at this stage.

The motor can now be turned on and (in the appropriate type of machine) the damping system alone turned on. A fine film of moisture should be visible on the plate except the image parts that will print. Next, the inking is turned on and ink allowed to build up on the image areas. Finally, all being well, the paper feed is turned on and the impression exerted — the paper is printed, the run begins.

The position of the printed image on the paper can be adjusted to fit the layout by moving the position of the paper stack. Likewise, to alter the position along the sheet, the printing plate cylinder can be adjusted: it is first unlocked and then turned by whatever amount is required, then re-locked, the details depending on the design of the machine.

Printing should now be straightforward, only the inking and damping arrangements requiring a little time to settle down.

In general, these machines are perfectly simple to operate and maintain; thousands of office juniors work them as part of their duties.

Of course, many things can go wrong, as with all mechanisms, from sewing machines to cars: we merely mention here a few of the commonest problems, which tend to perplex and discourage beginners.

Grey or spotty patches on blank parts of the print: probably a damping fault; check damping system is feeding properly to areas affected. Grey or spotty patches on the inked parts of the print: possibly a faulty plate or ink not reaching the area, but probably too much damping solution is being fed through and flooding the plate.

Blurred prints: possibly a loose plate or a loose 'blanket'. (The plate itself prints on to a rubber blanket wound on a second cylinder which itself transfers the image to the paper — hence the name offset printing as opposed to direct printing. This is why the plate is right-way-round whereas in letterpress the 'forme' is wrong-way-round.)

Paper feeding faults (eg two pages fed in at once): usually due to badly cut paper or paper not fanned out to free blurred edges before loading, or worn feeder fingers on a friction fed machine.

The machine *must* be cleaned carefully after use. Most inks will dry hard in a matter of hours and ruin the rollers, and the fount solution goes mouldy if left on. White spirit or similar cleaners or solvents are used for the rollers, and special formulations must be used on the blanket as it may have to be cleaned during the run, and the solvent must dry quickly. The proper instructions for cleaning a machine based on the delicate interaction of oily fluids and watery fluids must be obtained and adhered to.

Small offset machines are worked hard, and care must be used in buying one second-hand; the advice of an expert is worth getting. New desktop machines are expensive — costing up to £5,000, along with guarantees, servicing agreements and usually a week's training: but those who invest so much are really buying a commercial printshop rather than a home printing facility.

Photocopiers and computers

The development of photocopiers, home computers and word processors may be increasingly relevant to some home publishers and printers. At present expensive, the second-hand cost of these machines will inevitably fall. They are often available now as a side benefit of their purchase for some other purpose.

Photocopiers are limited to black and white reproduction, reproduce tones poorly, and currently use an expensive paper and cannot print on the verso; nor is register accurate. Older machines are expensive to maintain. But the next generation is overcoming these limitations, offering faster production, accurate lays, reduction and enlarging, availability of colour, and sheet collation also; and some can print on almost any paper. In time they may challenge litho as litho challenged letterpress.

Home computers and word processors offer several aids: word processing (which can be done on a special machine or on a general computer) allows novices to type without errors, and for texts to be amended, rearranged, justified, centred or re-set to different measures; the machine can completely re-type texts from its 'memory'. These facilities remove some drudgery from *some* writing, and editing, of texts. The usefulness of the final result depends on the device used to 'output'. For this many computers use poor quality 'dot-matrix' machines, but those with a daisywheel give respectable results. Some photosetting firms first 'capture' a text on floppy discs, or set it directly from them. The discs are used by the computer to store the text, which can then be prepared for printing by offset-litho, without further composition, in any form desired. There are already firms offering to photoset directly from a customer's own floppy discs for as little as £1.00 per 1,000 ens in a form ready for paste-up.

Home computers programmed to deal with the household accounts and business, which are entering homes in growing numbers, can, of course, handle a small publisher's accounts, send out bills, etc, very easily. This, no doubt, is the shape of all things to come.

Jean de Lemos

10

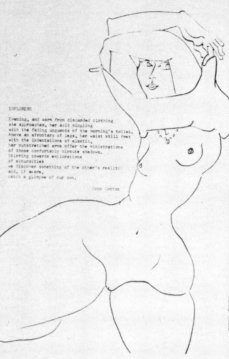

EXPLORERS

Evening, and warm from discarded clothing
she approaches, her acid mingling
with the fading unguents of the morning's toilet,
above an affrontery of legs, her waist still free
with the indentations of elastic.
her outstretched arms offer the ministrations
of those comfortably hirsute shadows.
Stirring towards explorations
of sinuosities
we discover something of the other's reality;
and, if aware,
catch a glimpse of our own.

John Cotton

KUDOS

Issue Eleven

Editor: Graham Sykes

Editorial Address: 7 Belle Vue Drive, Farsley, Pudsey,
W. Yorkshire, LS28 5HZ, England.

Price: 75p (plus 15p p&p)

Subscription Rates £3.00 UK (post free)
(four issues) £3.30 - £8.00 Overseas (post free)

Ads: £20 per page, £10 half page, £5 quarter.

Contributions: Poetry, fiction, articles, interviews,
translations and artwork of all kinds are welcomed for
consideration. These and all correspondence where a
reply is expected must be accompanied by s.a.e. or
international reply coupons sufficient to cover return.

Copyright (c) 1982 Graham Sykes.
Individual copyright rests with the author/artist.

Distributed with the assistance of the Yorkshire Arts
Association.

Financially supported by Leeds Arts Forum.

Printed by the Arc & Throstle Press, Todmorden, Lancs.

ISSN 0143 - 4969

8
THE MINORITY PERIODICAL

The duplicated magazine

Historically, books were printed for two centuries before news-sheets made their appearance. Technically, periodicals can be seen as ephemeral books in uniform format appearing at regular intervals — weekly, monthly, quarterly or annually. Logically, therefore, a discussion of the practicalities of minority-periodical publication follows that of hand-crafted books. Much of what we have said of the options for producing small editions applies to periodical publishing. However, there are differences. For example, while design is as important to periodical publishers as to book makers, our emphasis on good-quality paper hardly applies to periodicals; while binding is not a matter of *whether* but *where* staples are to be put in.

More amateurs start periodicals than decide to produce books or booklets. There is more familiarity with the home-made magazine, the first of which normally emerges from the children's den. Even so, the study of book publishing is a useful preliminary to bringing out a magazine or a periodical (or a 'fanzine'), which is in some ways easier but implies a regular routine.

Letterpress printing is no longer a serious option for home periodical production. Twenty-five years ago the school printing class or club used often to produce the school magazine, or the *alternative* school magazine. Seven boys with seven composing sticks could assemble quite substantial texts. Today the only recourse in letterpress is to get the text set in Linotype by a trade setter, which would be very expensive.

The usual method is the combination of typewriter, stencil and duplicator (p 85). This remains the cheap alternative to offset-litho. It is widely used for informal newsletters and magazines, usually in A4 format. But a long-carriage typewriter enables one to cut on the stencil two pages of A5 size which can then be stapled centrally, which is neater

(*opposite*) ────────────────────────────────
Plate 24 Varied magazine lay-outs using typewriter-originated text with various illustration techniques: (*top*) double-spread from *Kaleidoscope 3*, ed Jack Yates; (*bottom*) opening spread for *Kudos,* ed Graham Sykes

131

than A4 stapled down the edges of the sheets. It is possible for an (informal) artist to cut simple drawings on the stencil with an engraving tool, to be duplicated along with the text (p 170).

Such presentation techniques are not to be dismissed summarily, because they have a respectable history. Not a few have contributed to literature. *Priapus* magazine, run by John Cotton in the sixties, introduced not only poets like D. M. Thomas, Peter Jay, John Mole, Peter Scupham and Wes Magee, but artists Oscar Mellor, Rigby Graham and John Gilbert, all of whom now feature in top publishers' lists. Not a few magazines which started out in this unpretentious garb have grown into large-circulation journals because they identified an unfilled public need, like *Time Out.* Others became famous for different reasons, like Claud Cockburn's *The Week,* dedicated to the proposition that rumours are also facts in political affairs.

The stencil-and-mimeograph partnership suits the one-man journal and is likely to remain as much a voice in the contemporary scene as the one-man book publisher and printer.

But it is the advent of small offset that is responsible for the main growth in minority-magazine publishing. It has made possible the plethora of weekly newspapers rivalling or complementing the local press, and correcting their lapses from rectitude in publishing *all* the news, whether offensive or not to advertisers and County Hall.

A well-designed magazine printed by offset-litho has a better chance of attracting advertisements. Even the most high-minded journal can do with these, both for the extra revenue and as a signal to readers that the paper is substantial enough to attract the announcements of hardfisted businessmen. Adepts with dry transfer lettering can offer a service of display ads. A paper carrying ads, both classified and displayed, looks more solid than one without them; it is noteworthy that Mr Michael Horowitz's typewriter-originated and graphically inventive *New Departures* attracts some impressive top publishers' advertising. Its ideas and its bylines are too interesting for them to ignore.

In a quite different genre the magazine *Country Bazaar,* produced during the seventies by typewriter, graphics and offset-litho, with immense virtuosity in design, and comparable charm of content, was subsequently reproduced *in toto* as a large-format book by Astragal Books Ltd.

The periodical scene

We shall not give the attention to building circulation for a periodical that we did to marketing small editions. The literary magazine faces similar problems in getting subscribers and space on bookstalls. Most periodicals or organs of an institution are started by an individual or a group who already know the market they cater for and how to get at it. The magazine's policy defines it.

That policy can take many forms. It may be cultural: catering for a movement or clique within the arts. It may be defined by a religious group spreading their gospel. It may be scientific or technical, or concerned with a craft or lore, and addressed either to the neophytes or the adepts in that speciality, bringing like minds or interests into touch. It may be political, peddling a programme. It may be a guide to, or medium for, some sport, entertainment or collecting interest. In a changing world, the need springs up on all sides. Whatever its content, it should display continuity of line or of brief, emphasised by some uniformity of format, design, 'masthead' (title), cover graphic, or other livery. In this respect it differs entirely from the designing and publishing of the small edition.

For the home publisher is a law to himself. But the periodical is nearly always a group effort. Therefore it must have structure, leadership, delegation of jobs, however elementary such specialisation is. It requires a timetable and deadlines for receipt of copy, for origination of the edited copy, for delivery of that copy to the printer; it should have a publishing day of the week, month or whatever. Functions define themselves: the editor whose decision is final, the writing, editing and reporting operations, the origination and production; finally the distribution (possibly door-to-door), the advertising and 'space selling', the circulation and finance department.

It is not possible to generalise in such a variety of approaches. The timetable of a weekly, for example, may well begin with a first editorial conference (on content of next issue) on Monday morning, and the deadline for copy to printer (with an earlier deadline of copy to editor) may be Wednesday or Thursday, and so on for all the individual pages, especially if these are printed in succession. A daily paper usually has three editorial conferences a day, the last being at about 6pm (with perhaps a fourth with the night editor at 9pm). But its deadlines for the various pages and features will be complex, almost hourly, and varied according to each page. The timetable of even the most informal periodical will emerge if one works backwards from publication day and from the time the printer (whether he is at home or is a commercial printshop) wants last copy.

We are reminded of a weekly, tabloid-sized 12-page newspaper serving a certain county in Maine, USA, which we visited some years ago. The wife was editor and reporter and, en route as it were, ad space saleswoman. The husband was compositor, lay-out and paste-up man, while the third member (adult) of the family helped out with the feature

133

Written and illustrated by **Elliot Rudie**

The following three poems form part of a longer sequence, dedicated to the city of Dundee. Unfortunately, due to lack of space, we are unable to include the whole series.

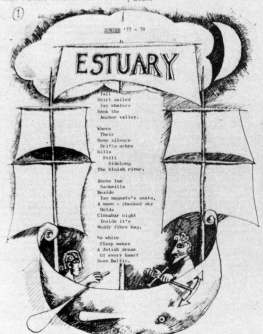

Brian Patten   (b. 1946, Liverpool)

No. No thank you, but no. No. Not just yet.
Later, perhaps some other time.
Maybe in a few moments. Maybe tomorrow.
Thankyou but no. No, I'm afraid not.
No I really can't. I might but, but no,
I'm dreadfully sorry. If only . . . but no.
No, it is a pity but
if things were different I might
The problem is I'm unable to I'm
No. No I couldn't. I can't. I'm afraid that
if, but, no, honestly, no.

When you think of things that are lost that you wish
    to find again,
of the bodies that leapt as if touch were both release
    and frightening trap,
you can be sure No will cloud your ambitions.
When you wonder why there are things the tongue
    can no longer haul up from the soul,
you'll find it in No that weighs them down.
When you hear a miracle complain of its ordinariness
    you can be sure it's been listening to No -

For no comes sneaking through the blood,
No comes in fancy clothes to sew up the eyelids,
With its retinue of doubts it clambers up onto the soul
and squats there like a goblin.
It's got a fat bagful of reasons,
an excuse for everything.

How lovely it would be to be cured of No . . .

Eh? What? Me?
Take the cure? Try? Me?
No.. No thankyou, but no. No not just yet.
Later. Perhaps some other time. Maybe in a few moments.
Maybe tomorrow. No. I'm afraid not. No. No not just now.

30

Heathcote Williams   (Wales -- b. 41, Helsby, Cheshire)

Death is Taboo but there's no Taboo against Dying · *Death* defaces you to your Face · *Death* Chain smokes all Forms of Life · *Death* floods your Meat with Adrenalin so that you're inedible · *Death* trains you as a Guard Dog from Birth so you won't kill it · *Death* stockpiles the Chemistry of your Smiles · *Death* drains the Fuck out of you to let low Spirits in and use your Body as a Coffin · *Death* is the Paranoiac's only Hope · *Death* treats World Wars like a Line of good Coke · *Death* gets high on *Death* · *Death* is when you stop listening to your inner Voice for so long that it stops listening to you · *Death* is using your Imagination out of Despair and not Desire · *Death* is when every Stimulus contracts your Mind · *Death* is a Conspiracy of Kaka Consciousness · *Death* is when other People's Body Clocks strike the Hour every Minute · *Death* is Passion being Drip fed to Sentiment · *Death* is for failed Suicides · *Death* is when your Eyes blink and take Photographs but you know the Developer's gone stale · *Death* is being greedy to have all your Pain at once · *Death* digs you deeper than Anyone · *Death* is worrying other People into the Force Field of your own Extinction · *Death* fucks you up and down · *Death* fills your Spirit Level with Marsh Gas · *Death* is the Life and Soul of all political Parties · *Death* watches you fuck yourself off and then get Lockjaw · *Death* is ungrateful for all the Fear that's lavished on it ·
Death is the hardest Asana in Yoga

DEATH IS UNSPEAKABLE

writing, advertising and everything that needed an extra hand. This simple organisation, housed in a typical wooden-frame New England home, was centred upon the hire-purchase of a phototypesetting composer which made possible the swift composition of text and headlines of the entire contents (apart from overmatter and specials) in two days of the week. The composer continued to earn its hire charges by being under lease for two other days to another family producing another weekly in another county on another day of the week; while on Saturdays it was kept busy churning out the texts of local-history booklets that they wrote themselves. On Sunday they went to church where they met many of their subscribers and advertisers and collected news and criticisms for the next issue. The printing was done by an offset-litho printshop in a nearby town from the paste-ups; its machinery also folded, wrapped, addressed and franked the copies for mailing. There was no trouble with trade unions.

Production

As with books, the first stage in planning a new periodical is design. This, though flexible, will be replicated issue by issue in page size, typography, headline treatment, layout, and ornament. As with books, when planning a new periodical there is everything to be said for a critical appraisal of similar magazines, whether commercial (can we do nearly as well?) or amateur (can we do better?). This is important when deciding what sort of a message will interest what sort of public. The analysis should consider page-size, number of pages, words per page — and per column if layout is columnar — method of production, paper, use of colour, and so on, always with the thought, 'How did they do it and at what cost?'.

Nobody can expect to produce anything rivalling the *New Yorker*'s *dégagé* chic; but much is to be learned from studying its layout — for instance its skilled use of casual ornament as both fillers and relief to weight of text. (Much can be learned from its English style!) The skill with which *Private Eye* uses unjustified typewritten text within column rules combined with dry transfer lettering headlines in Victorian styles to effect a flavour of the off beat and improvised, is no less worthy of consideration. But while layout and production can do much, what actually *sells* a periodical is its content.

(opposite) —————————————————————————————

Plate 25 Use of arresting layouts and texts by the 'little magazines': *(top)* typewriting and hand-lettering combined with graphics from *Logos* (ed A. Keithley) of Scotland; *(bottom)* calligraphy, typewriting and drawings combined in *New Departures* (ed Michael Horowitz, Gloucestershire)

135

The decision on design will shape a dummy: this is a vital preliminary when launching a new commercial magazine. It is shown to potential advertisers — indeed a 'dry run' is often fully printed off in a few copies for this purpose.

Once the dummy and layout have been finalised a stage intervenes which is unnecessary when making a book. It is to prepare and print a stock of 'make up' sheets onto which the texts, headlines and graphics of the magazine can be pasted. It is usual to have the margins and column measures printed in pale blue (so that the camera does not reproduce them). The column divider rules must be put in later in black because headlines, etc, may cross two columns. If each page is boxed in a black rule, as was common in the nineteenth century and is now quite fashionable again, this can be printed in black on the make-up (or as they are also called 'lay-out') sheets. If the periodical is very informal, it will be possible to rule the make-up sheets by hand; either way such sheets are indispensable.

The make-up sheets at once standardise the appearance of a periodical and facilitate the process of pasting-up the originated text, which is usually supplied by the printer or the typist set to the prescribed measure on strips of paper. If the layout of the magazine is complex, it is convenient to have several typical layouts pre-printed in blue on alternative make-up sheets. The same object may be attained by ruled overlays on tracing paper, so that the various layouts can be blocked in by pencil on the make-up sheets.

Essentially the approach to lay-out must be modular. This is simple if the layout is 'longitudinal', keeping the text in almost unbroken columns, as was suitable to letterpress methods. This is now voted dull, and the 'horizontal' design is usual, with headlines breaking through columns — double and triple column headlines, with features dotted about in 'boxes' (rectangles enclosed in rules) and so forth. Such designs readily lend themselves to offset-litho printing techniques.

The appearance of the paper will depend on the accuracy with which the paste-up department has done its job in arranging the elements of text, graphics and headlines and pasting them firmly and squarely down. All that was said on this subject in Chapter 7 applies. Organisation becomes vital — the organisation of the drafting table. The paste-up man or woman will be surrounded with bits of copy of all shapes and sizes (and if he loses one of these it must be re-originated). It is best to number each item on its back, and the space it is to occupy, and to build up sub-assemblies of complex items prior to final positioning on the make-up sheet.

Another advantage of the pre-printed make-up sheet is that the margins can be calibrated in column inches, and a note kept of the average number of words (or characters) that a column-inch will accommodate, including the space taken up by the various styles of headings, etc. By this means the stage of 'copy-fitting' is much facilitated. Every article or other item is cast off (measured) in the usual way; the number of words immediately shows how many column inches it will make. The sum may be done again after it has been sub-edited and cut. With the standard allowance for the headline, the total space it will take up on the page can then be known in advance, which will ease the problem at paste-up.

In essence this is the whole procedure, but it may be a complicated one when graphics, half-tones, tabular matter, maps, display advertisements and so on all have to be fitted onto a page of the lay-out. It corresponds to the elaborate lay-outs demanded by certain profusely-illustrated scientific or art books — only, it must be regularly done to tight deadlines.

Origination

The options for setting the text of a periodical are much the same as for a book. But an unjustified right-hand margin is more acceptable in a magazine; indeed commercial 'glossies' alternate between justified and unjustified text settings simply to vary their appearance. However, typewritten copy does not fit very well into columnar design because the narrowness of the columns imposes either greater raggedness on the right-hand margin, or uncanonical word-breaks. The average newspaper column is about 2½ inches or 15 picas, which accommodates 48 characters or about five words in 8-point type, but only 21 characters or 3½ words in 12-pitch typewriter type. As with books, it is possible to have the camera-ready artwork reduced by process camera for platemaking, but in a complex lay-out, in which every other element must be reduced pro rata, this means problems for the inexperienced.

We feel the best alternative at present is the Varityper, described in more detail on pp 22–3. Its mechanism permits a quick change in type size as well as in typeface — roman to italic to bold, highly desirable if the periodical is of newspaper design. Though much more expensive than a typewriter, the Varityper is rather cheaper than an electronic composer and is probably easier for the amateur to operate and maintain. For a magazine editor with tabular matter and mathematical settings to accommodate, it has advantages which may be decisive, although, like the IBM Executive typewriter, it is no longer manufactured; one is dependent on reconditioned models (mainly advertised in *Exchange and Mart*).

For many magazines the best method of origination is the electronic

137

composer, whether 'strike-on', or photographic. When the setting can be compressed into a short period, it may be practicable to hire one for that period. It is unlikely to be possible for a weekly paper. It is not always or everywhere possible to get a weekly hire contract. It becomes more feasible for monthly magazines.

For publishers who have the resources to have their magazines printed in their entirety by a commercial printer, the guidelines for relations and contract mentioned in Chapter 4 may serve. The additional factor is of course the necessity of agreeing with the printer delivery dates for (a) handing in subbed copy, correctly marked up, for setting; (b) for receipt of galley proofs; (c) for returning corrected galley proofs along with layouts for imposition (make-up); (d) for printing to distribution deadline. It is still advisable, when using an outside printer, to have preprinted make-up sheets on which a spare set of galleys is pasted to show (for his convenience) the approximate 'fall' of the copy; corrections are of course sent in on separate sets of galleys. Final adjustments are usually made when the page proofs of the magazine are read, at the printer's offices in the case of a weekly paper, and even a monthly. The fewer these final adjustments, the smaller the printer's bill.

As with the production of books by offset-litho, it is open to the magazine publisher to cut costs by doing some of the production himself, and subcontracting out portions of the magazine to the printer. Here are seven variants of the division of functions between the home and the local commercial printshop.

	Origination		Paste-up	Printing	Folding/	Distribution
	of text	of display			finishing	
1	put out	put out	put out	put out	put out	put out*
2	put out	put out	home	put out	put out	home
3	put out	home	home	put out	put out	home
4	put out	home	home	put out	home	home
5	home	home	home	put out	home	home
6	put out	home	home	home**	home	home
7	home	home	home	home**	home	home

*Mailing from printer's office, as opposed to personal or group door-to-door distribution. **There is a further option of putting out the platemaking only.

In general, as with books, the least expensive way to use a printer's services are to contract with him to do the setting — which is important if a periodical is weekly, as trade setters can provide a 24-hour service — and printing; everything else can be done 'in-house'.

Newspapers and news-magazines will naturally require display type in many more varieties and sizes than the simple uses for them in book production (145). This will additionally be so if a home-produced journal accepts and undertakes to compose display advertisements. Not only is this quite expensive, but also it involves much more complex paste-ups. It is advisable to obtain one of the special manuals on elaborate and specialised paste-ups designed for the DIY trade as well as for experts; it would take us much space to provide a full exposition which would be of use to only a few readers. Part of the fun, in any event, of running one's own periodical is to learn the interesting effects that can be achieved with the new techniques, quite simply and inexpensively, once one has become familiar with their manifold applications. This is true of the use of stencils and duplicators as well as lithography.

In the production of periodicals, as of books, there is frequently a good reason for using a small letterpress plant, or co-operating with a small jobbing sparetime printer, to get proofs on 'repro' paper of display items or assemblies for incorporation in the paste-up. If speed is essential, there are obvious advantages in having such an adjunct under one's own control.

We have tried to give timings for the various operations involved in book publishing. It is almost impossible to do so for periodical publication. Usually people who start magazines find that they take up far more time than was expected. Here is a rough time budget for the production time (*not* the editorial time) spent on a well-displayed magazine consisting of 24 pages of A5 size (6 A4 sheets) and coloured cover.

		Hours	
Text setting (by IBM composer) mostly unjustified right-hand margins		12	
Repro pulls for display (headings, sub-heads, decorative panels, cover design etc) from letterpress settings		10	
Paste-up of pages, 1 hour per spread		12	
	Artwork		32
Negatives of half-tones, two pages		1	
Negatives, line, all pages		2	
Spotting out negatives etc		2	
Plates made from negatives		2	
	Platemaking		7
Setting up machines for single-colour run		1	
Running pages (13 runs of 3,000 copies at 2,000 an hour)		20	
	Machining		21

Gathering, folding, stapling, 200 copies per hour
Trimming stapled copies, 800 per hour.

139

An indispensable requirement of a periodical enterprise is the accurate record of subscribers, both paid-up and unpaid-up. Sale of a book is a single transaction. But a subscriber to a magazine pays in advance, and the publisher is contractually bound to deliver to him the issues that he has paid for, or refund his money if these cannot be produced for some reason. If all or most of the money is paid in advance upon the issue of number 1 for six succeeding issues, it is simple to calculate that the total receipts must be divided by six to see if each issue is paying its way. But if subscriptions are coming in and running out unrenewed at various times, and there is advertisement revenue to take into the account, a very careful running record of receipts, expenses and future obligations must be kept to ensure that there will be enough in the bank to finance later issues for which money by subscribers (and advertisers) has been received; if not, there will be debtors to pay off. This is self-evident, but not everyone who starts a magazine in the high spirit of faith quite grasps the financial implications of doing so.

9
LETTERPRESS PRINTING

Time versus money

The alternative to small offset is traditional letterpress printing. This was once the only way to produce a book or pamphlet at home. The basic simplicity of the process is shown by the hundreds of self-taught non-experts who did so.

Some of them followed the very oldest traditions of the craft and constructed their presses, cases, etc, themselves, confining money outlay to type and a few 'ironmonger's items'. Schools' carpentry classes were expected to do as much and instruction manuals are available.

Printing on such a shoe-string excepted, people who decide on letter-press expect to buy a complete plant. The table on pp 158–9 gives a rough comparison of the costs of acquiring second-hand small offset and letterpress equipment.

Letterpress comes out far cheaper. On the other hand, it is far slower. Much of the history of printing in the nineteenth century was the search for fast, mechanical methods of composing type. Eventually the Lino-type and Monotype systems emerged. As offset-lithography has taken over (except in Fleet Street) these machines have been scrapped in large numbers and can be bought cheaply. Some amateurs have acquired them. However, a Linotype stands nine feet high and weighs tons. The Monotype comprises two machines of even greater complexity, one that casts and one with a keyboard for composing — it works by compressed air as well as electricity. Getting such machines maintained is increasingly difficult. Most owners of a letterpress plant will have to be content with the methods of hand-setting which produced all the printed books in the world from 1460 to around 1890.

So the key question is: how long does it take to set up a page in type by hand? A skilled compositor used to set 2,000–3,000 ens an hour, about 350–450 words, or a page of prose 18 picas (3½ inches) wide by 30 picas (5½ inches) deep. Assuming that the amateur can do half the expert's average speed, he can set 150 words an hour, so that a page will take him two to three hours. To this must be added half to threequarters of an hour to re-distribute the type into the case for re-use. Poetry takes approximately two-thirds of that time.

Hence a booklet of eight pages of prose will call for some 14 to 18 hours of setting — not, of course, continuous hours, one can do a little or a lot at odd times, like knitting.

It is a formidable comparison with the typewriting options. But there is no question of the superiority of the appearance of letterpress.

The owners of letterpress plants can, and many do, compromise by getting their long texts set for them by a trade typesetter with a Linotype, or Monotype. The type is set and hired to the printer who is credited with the cost of metal, less drossage, when he has printed from ·it. In 1983, including loss by drossage, it cost from £1.70 to 4.00 per 1,000 ens (150 words) to get type set by Linotype, which is not much more, if any more, than having text set by a commercial setter on an IBM composer for offset-litho reproduction. Monotype setting cost a third as much more. Such bought-out settings can be printed along with one's own case type for headings, etc, and indeed for text.

How much type?

Type is expensive when bought new. What therefore is the minimum one needs? That of course depends on the sort of books to be printed. The bare minimum is enough to set one page, of the wordage the publisher-printer decides upon. Some specialised books require little wordage per page. For a page of 250 words a standard fount of 8lb of 10- or 12-point type would be needed, and supplemented with a smaller ('card') fount of italic. To this would be added 3lb of spaces to put between words, and 'leads' to space out the lines. In 1983 the total cost would be £50 for brand-new type and spaces. Second-hand this amount could be bought for perhaps £10 or £12 (but see below).

Such minimum resources for hand-setting assumes that the book is to be printed one page at a time. This is possible, and has often been done. The simplicity of the hand presses shown in Plate 33 lends itself to such a procedure, because the paper can be inserted in differing positions and can protrude sideways from the jaws of the mechanism. One can then set one page, print it on the recto as page 1; distribute the type, set page 2, and print it to back page 1 on the verso of the sheet, and so proceed page by page, working according to the dummy and layout. The two objections are that a complete set of proofs cannot be sent to an author; and it becomes a bit of a bore inking, preparing the machine and washing up after every page run. It is quicker to print off pages in batches.

However, a home printer with plenty of time and careful designing and preplanning can print books this way at a minimum cost. Moreover he can print them in sheets of four pages quite easily, and perfect-bind them in the way explained in Fig 9 on p 79. Or he can print inner and

142

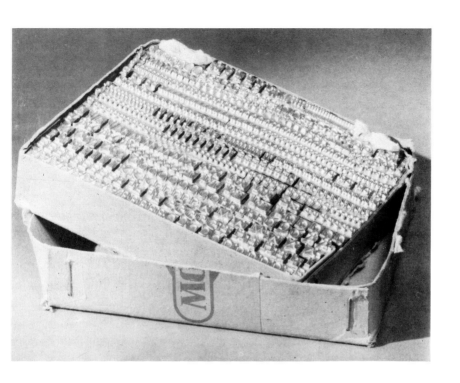

AAAAAAAABBBBBC ꞇC ꞇC DDDDDEE
EEEEEEEEF ꜰF ꜰF GGGGGH ʜH ʜH ɪI ɪ
I ɪI ɪI J J J J KKKLLLLLM ᴍM ᴍM ɴ ɴ-
N ɴN ɴN ɴOOOOOO OOPPPPPQ ꞯQ ꞯ ꞯ-
R ꞯR ꞯR ꞯSSSSSSSST ᴛT ᴛT ᴛT ᴛUUUUU
V ᴧV ᴧWWWWWX ꭓX ꭓY ꭓY ᴢZ aaaaaaa
aaaaaaaaaabbbbbbbbcccccccccccddddddddddddeeeeee
eeeeeeeeeeeeee ſ ſ ſ ſ ſ ſ ſ ſ gggggggghhhhhhhhhhhi
iiiiiiiiiiiii j j j j j ꝗk ꝗk ꝗllllllllllll mmmmmmmmmmnn
nnnnnnnnnnnnnnnnnooooooooooooooooooooood pd pd p-
ꝺ bq bq rrrrrrrrrrrrrrrrrrssssssssssssssssssssssttttttttt
ttttttttttuuuuuuuuuvvvvvvvwwwwwwwwwwwxxxxx
yyyyyyyzzzz1111222333444555666777888999 0
0 0 0 ꝆꝆꞒꞒ ꜲꜲ ꜱꜱꜱ ꜳꜳꜳ ꝰꝰ & & & $$QQ ﬀﬂﬃ
? ɥ ﬁ ﬀ ﬀ ﬂ ﬂ ! ! ”” ; : : ,,,,,,,,,,,........?

Plate 26 A fount of (display) type as received from the supplier and a proof (Fig 27) showing
composition of characters

143

outer sheets to make sections of 8 or 12 pages if he follows his dummy and layout very closely and makes sure the type area is correct on each page.

However, most private presses like to machine two pages at a time, and hold as their body fount enough type to set five pages at a time at least. Then they can set five pages of an 8-page section outright, and by printing off the inner sheets first, and distributing the type, they can set the other three pages and then run the rest of the 8-page section continuously. Authors sometimes find it odd that their proofs come five or six pages at a time — but after all the first folio of Shakespeare's plays, scholars tell us, was printed only 12 pages at a time as there was not enough type for more than that amount of setting.

The cost of type to operate on this more comfortable scale will not be less than £200 if bought new. There are various ways of calculating how much type to buy for a given amount of text. Typefounders sell new type in founts of 8 or 10lb (or kilo equivalents), and indicate how many capital A's and lower-case a's each fount of each typeface and size contains. All other letters, signs, points etc, are supplied in due proportion for use in the English language. It is thus possible roughly to calculate how many words can be set from a given number of A's and a's. As a rough rule, a occurs once in every three words in English. So a fount with 100 a's in it will set 300 words, thereabouts, depending on peculiarities of the text. This does not mean that the fount will be set completely out — about a third of the type will be left unused in the case for any particular text.

If an 8lb fount with 100 a's, etc, is insufficient, it is possible to buy an additional half-fount of lower-case letters only, usually doubling the wordage capacity of the combined weight of type. If extra letters are needed for a special text, these are bought as 'sorts', but are charged twice the fount rate.

Many will think, therefore, in terms of second-hand type. But it must be bought with care. It is not sold in properly assorted cartons, but already distributed in cases, and it may be that the case is deficient in the quantities of some 'sorts'; so the amounts of type, in the major boxes, e's, a's, h's and so on, have to be checked. So has the wear on the type: unevenly worn type is harder to print, even if one seeks an old-world effect! So one has usually to buy more second-hand type by weight, to achieve the same wordage as new type in standard founts. Even so, it is a worthwhile option, as it can be bought at less than a third of the price of new type.

As the quantity of type held is increased, so also, of course, must be the quantity of spaces and leads, but these can readily be used when second-hand.

144

What sort of type?

The sparetime printer making a supplementary income by printing business or social stationery needs a variety of type sizes and styles, but in limited quantities of each. A book printer needs only one type face, in perhaps two sizes, but his 'body fount' has to be substantial, 12 to 24lb in weight — a full standard double case (Plate 27). If he invests in a substantial amount of italic also, he will virtually have two faces to ring the changes on. The variations possible in a single typeface are shown in Fig 14 on p 92.

Both on grounds of economy and style, we join with other writers in recommending adherence to a single typeface; it is far better to have substantial amounts in one face, than several ill-assorted faces in founts capable only of setting half a paragraph. The golden rule for fast composition: have all you need to hand and plenty of it.

Given that a publisher sticks to one face, which face should it be? Typefounders' catalogues offer a bewildering variety to the novice. One way to choose is to find books which are to one's taste, match the typeface used in them to the typefounder's catalogue and settle for it. It will almost certainly be one of a dozen well-known and well-tried 'book faces'; we illustrate a few in Fig 19 on p 103. Of course, if there is money to lavish, one can indulge one's fancies.

A bad typeface can spoil the appearance of a book, but in general it is the design of a book, not the particular typeface used, that is decisive. It is true that certain faces suit certain texts more than others; but, considering what typewriter type faces look like, it is a minor point for all but publishers with plenty of money. Any standard typeface can be varied by leading out the lines, and suiting the typographical layout to the page, margins, paper quality, etc.

The standard faces have the advantage that reasonably compatible versions are available in Monotype, Linotype, photosetting, and even 'golf ball' or 'daisywheel' founts fitted to electronic strike-on composers. This is useful when one decides to have the text set outside, or possibly partly printed by a different method from other parts of the book produced at home.

Composition by hand

Many manuals describing the process of typesetting, imposition, and machining exist, beginning with Moxon's classic of 1680 (see Bibliography). Here we can give only an outline of the minimum skill needed in small-book work. The art of printing beautiful books cannot be compressed into a few pages — but anyone who sets up a printshop will soon

145

Plate 27 Double case of type showing different-sized compartments for frequently used and less-used lower-case characters, or 'sorts'. It holds 25lb of type

Plate 28 A 'dressed' chase, showing how quoins apply pressure from two sides and how wood furniture is used to fill space between chase and type and spread the quoins' pressure

Plate 29 'Furniture and reglet' cut to standard sizes in picas: metal, wood and plastic varieties

Plate 30 Tools and accessories for dressing the chase: mallet and planer (to smooth surface of type), brush for cleaning, varieties of mechanical quoins and their keys, wood quoins and 'shooting stick' to drive them home

want to learn typography and its finer points. Here we confine ourselves to basics, partly with the aim of assuring the reader that almost anyone can do it; a craft 500 years old can be mastered by any intelligent person with some manual dexterity.

Furthermore, experience in the basics of letterpress printing is an education in design itself — just as learning to manage a small boat is of value to those who intend to navigate ships by radar and little else!

The first step is to grasp the characteristics of the metal type, spaces, 'quads' and leads used to build up a page of text, and the 'furniture' used to hold the mass of type so built up in the iron frame, the 'chase', which in turn is placed against the bed of the printing press for inking and printing (Plates 27–30 and Figs 28 and 29).

Type is picked from the case and placed against a lead or brass rule in the composing stick, a three-sided tray with an adjustable side to fit any measure. The nick in the type enables all the letters to be set the same way round. The setting is, of course, upside-down and left to right (ie as seen in a mirror), so that when printed it is read left to right. A little experience in setting soon accustoms the human eye to this. The thumb holds the type in position (Plate 31).

The typecase carries spaces in five widths, twelve different combinations, to separate words in such a way that the line can be made to fit the measure precisely (see p 89). The compositor's skill is essentially the ability to make this fit, so that when the line is complete, and tilted away from the compositor, the line just remains upright; if all the lines are so justified, the mass of type when locked in the chase will lift perfectly and become a single solid under pressure.

Beginners are advised to put leads between their lines of type. After the first line is made to fit, a lead is put against it and a second line begun. After four lines or so have been set they must be moved from the stick to the galley, or to the dressed chase, in the place required by the layout. Plate 31 shows how this is done, and how a complete set of pairs of pages is built up, line by line.

Let us now run through the procedure of preparing eight pages for printing in the same order, and with exactly the same result, as we did in summarising the way of preparing a paste-up of an eight-page pamphlet for offset printing (p 113). A single page is illustrated first (Plate 28) to show the full detail of a filled chase, 'locked up' by quoins

(*opposite*) ————————————————————————————————————
Plate 31 How to set type: (*top left*) holding the composing stick and picking up letter, feeling for the 'nick'; (*top right*) changing a space to make the line fit the width of the measure; (*bottom left*) removing set lines from the stick (note the leads supporting top and bottom of the type and finger pressuring the sides; (*bottom right*) transferring the type in the fingers to the galley (or directly to a dressed chase)

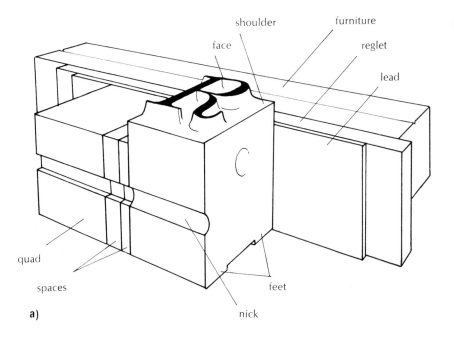

quad

spaces

feet

nick

a)

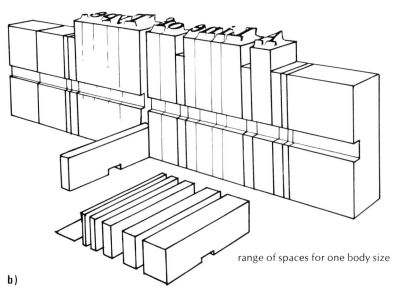

range of spaces for one body size

b)

Fig 28 Metal type: (a) the parts of a separate piece of type; (b) a line of type, spaces and quads or large spaces, and the range of widths of spaces available for increasing/reducing space between words to make lines fit the measure exactly (or wedges). It makes life easier to have four chases, each dressed to receive the type in the proper order, just like a make-up sheet laid out with blue-pencilled margins to receive the pages of typed text as shown in Plate 19.

In the chases, the furniture of wood or metal (Plate 29) is arranged to give the margins laid down in the dummy, measured in points, and is in fact an exact replica of the design, but reversed and in three dimensions. Space is left at the top and sides for quoins to tighten the formes. (If the pages are first built up in galleys, the compositor must transfer them from galleys to chases in proper order — as professional printers normally do.) The furniture round each chase must be identical (it is cheap and one can have plenty).

As will be seen, the first chase contains the type for pages 1 and 8. The compositor leaves the space for page 8 empty while he fills the space for page 2, and so on, working round the chases, and filling the space for page 8 last. Then the chases are locked up by the quoins and proofs can be taken, either on the press itself, or by the simple method of inking the type, placing paper on it, and on that a piece of wood round which is wrapped a rubber backing or felt, and tapping it with a mallet.

To make the corrections, the chases have to be returned to the imposing surface again, unlocked, and tweezers employed to remove the wrong letters, and replace them by the right ones. Adjustments to spaces have to be made, obviously, if an m is to be replaced by an l. The line may have to be eased out and replaced in the stick for extensive respacing and correcting. It is far easier to make corrections when *setting* the type than *after* it has been imposed. So the compositor should read every line after he has set it in the stick. It will save hours, perhaps.

If the pages are printed in fours, one needs only two chases, and the imposition is correspondingly simpler.

It is a simple procedure which can be done in stages at odd times if preferred. It is quicker than may appear, because, with everything under one's own roof and control, one is not fitting oneself to a printer's time and exigencies; one works at weekends and in evenings, and soon learns one's own short cuts and unorthodoxies — what we have proposed is ruthlessly unorthodox anyway. A good book on letterpress printing methods will be an ever-present help in difficulty and doubt.

(overleaf)

Fig 29 The corresponding printed pages of the type in the dressed chases shown in Plate 32 and corresponding to the artwork for litho plates shown in Fig 21

Plate 32 A set of eight book pages imposed in four chases, each with two pages. Note use of equal widths of furniture, and quoins space, to ensure matching margins

St. George and the Dragon

ᴍANY YEARS AGO there lived a young man called George who was so determined to become a saint if he possibly could. At that period it was ... reasonable ambition. Up to a score of saints were around at any one time, converting pagans to Christianity and performing minor miracles such as walking on water when the bridges were down between them and the pagans scheduled to be converted.

George had hoped to take holy orders for this very purpose, but from boyhood he had evinced outstanding skill in the handling of horses, arms and armour. He won all his jousts, and in our day, would have become an international sportsman. Quite why those were the days when gifted young people went to such lengths for sainthood, but he was content to try for sainthood. He did achieve ... if tardy, ... of the talents God had given him and become

[page 1]

---

a knight-errant. Regrettably he consecrated. There seemed much less chance of getting to be a saint that way, but he manfully resolved to work his way up from the bottom rung of the ladder.

He had little difficulty in resolving temptations which were **2** supposed to ... him become a ... eagerly offered ... Instead he rode about on his horse rescuing people from distress — mainly from robbers and wild beasts, occasionally from sorcerers. He acquired quite a reputation for his sort of thing, and barons leaned on him to galled all over their domains, performing constabulary duties in full armour.

He liked the work. Most of all, he enjoyed rescuing virgins from a fate worse than death at the hands of outlaws, or, failing that, from common or garden death in the jaws of wolves or lions. He was kept busy, because in those days there were many more virgins than there now are, and they were perpetually getting into difficulties and requiring rescue by knights-errant. Quite why, is not made clear by contemporary chroniclers.

This George was certainly collecting credits, but they hardly added up to sainthood. He did ...

[page 2]

Christianity whiler armed *cap-à-pied*, but this obviously did not rate with missionary work done only with a crozier.

Eventually, however, he arrived in a town whose inhabitants were being terrorized by a dragon, and they were buying it off by supplying it with a virgin to eat every Sunday. Why it had to be a virgin, **3** either historians have put forward var ... obBesses, and arri ... monious have been t ... ng controversies. However the townsfolk reached their decision in this matter, the event fully justified it.

For it lest George on his mettle. He was enthusiastic over the rescue of the current virgin — a prospect even more in the line than if the virgin had been a fair young, or married lady. And he had never fought a dragon before, having supposed them to be extinct for some years — it added professional interest to the prospect. He had to overawe only his armour and the tracks of the dragon who had crawled back to his lair to digest his dinner.

They were naturally disappointed. A week later they prepared to tie up a virgin according to schedule—the same one. But she escaped her fate again. A terrible stench proclaimed that the dragon was dead. After a regular diet of tender virgins his digestion had completely broken

[page 3]

"I surrender, noble knight, to superior force!" And he rolled over on his back, exposing his soft underbelly. It would not have been sporting, or, as George would have phrased it, chivalrous, to kill it like that. So he rode up and demanded to know why the dragon would not put up a fight.

"You're too strong," said the dragon. "Despatch me, if you will **4** r it. But you better untie that girl and s some first."

"Why?" asked Gi uzzled.

"So she doesn't see what child's play it was for you to do in a poor, damn, helpless animal," said the dragon. "Then you can go back and tell them about the frightful battle we had, and how you nearly lost your life, and you'll be acclaimed as a hero."

"I don't pretend to be a hero, and I don't behave like that," said George reprovingly. "I hope to be a saint. My life means nothing to me so long as I lose it doing God's work."

"Oh, I see," said the dragon. "In that case you certainly ought to fight bravely against all odds and slay me, for I am pre-Christian, prehistoric and all that. But I don't see how I can give you a decent fight. You could make it more equal by taking off your armour, I suppose. I have no armour. Look at my soft underbelly."

[page 4]

"Why, that's true enough," replied George, much struck by this point. Having armour on was really an unfair advantage, and, now that he came to think of it, always had been. Robbers and lions were no more encased in steel than dragons. What merit could there be in killing them? "I shall take it off!" he announced, and proceeded to do so. **5** the dragon. "But you've got a horse, v is you've six legs and two arms to my tour.

"Don't worry, I shall dismount," said George. "I'll end this dear girl home on my steed. Then nobody can say I won and with victory heroic feat. God is my witness—I need no other!" And he sent in his tittol darned off.

"Bravo, brave knight! I can smell the odour of sanctity already," said the dragon, licking its chops. "Still, you know, I have only my teeth,

[page 5]

---

which are of primitive design, while you have a blade of Damascus steel, and a battle-axe, and a mace, and a lance, and a nifty little Assyrian bow for emergencies *and* a deadly dagger in reserve. If you really want to fight fair, you'll choose a single weapon—of course I am not suggesting you rely on your teeth, beautifully white and even as th

"Any weapon will **6** h God's-strength behind it," cried Geo choose whichever you prefer to die of."

"The dagger," said the dragon quickly.

"On guard!" roared George.

The contest did not last long. Old as the dragon was, it had led George before he could make even one lunge with his dagger, and ate him up.

The townsfolk, alerted by the virgin, had marched out to see how their champion had got on. They found only his armour and the tracks of the dragon who had crawled back to his lair to digest his dinner.

[page 6]

---

down on the solid bone (especially on the skull bone) and knotted musculature of George. For once the dragon had been too clever by half.

The townsfolk were overjoyed and those of them who were still pagan ... at once converted. The miracle was claimed as a great cavalry by the Church, and the Church, not in need of money) had little option but **7** to ... George a saint.

The artists preferred to commemorate him in full armour symbolically piercing the dragon's soft underbelly with his lance, the difficulties of depicting a knight slaying a dragon by giving it indigestion proved too great for the technique of the time. Ultimately the artist's version was taken as a literal record.

Not, however, for some time. The real story persisted for several centuries, and where it was told to him that led him, cleric of England, in the course of one of its many journeys to the Danes, he clapped his hands with delight and decided to

[page 7]

---

adopt St. George as patron saint of England.

"He will be an inspiration to us all, and to succeeding generations no less," said the King. "Let us disarm unilaterally, for we are without doubt lethally indigestible to any conqueror."

Somewhat later the Church, going over its extensive archive **8** e a lot unhappy about George's record, noted him from saint-hood. I understand ad nothing to do with concern for England, nor were any suggestions put forward for an alternative patron saint.

[page 8]

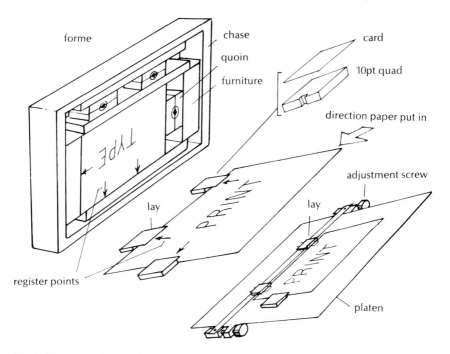

Labels on figure: forme, chase, card, quoin, 10pt quad, furniture, direction paper put in, adjustment screw, TYPE, lay, PRINT, lay, PRINT, register points, platen

Fig 30 Diagrams showing how paper is positioned on the platen of a letterpress printing machine to achieve the desired 'register', margins etc; three points of register are needed as shown to match with the fixed edges of the type area. Some machines have adjustable 'lays', as shown

When purchasing letterpress equipment, it is worth while to think out in advance the main *measures* one is likely to want for one's book — for example, lines 3 or 3½ inches (18 or 21 picas) long. Then all furniture, reglet and leads can be cut to these sizes only (or at least, initially). The standard measure can always be made smaller by setting an em at the beginning of the lines. Such standardisation and simplification of the operation will keep costs to a minimum.

Press and printing machine

It is usual to recommend to people setting up a printing plant first to decide what they mean to print and then buy a machine capable of it. This is sound, subject to the machines being available. Most printing machines are second-hand nowadays, though there are plenty to choose from. We illustrate the main types of small printing machines in Plate 33. For book production, the larger and heavier presses are obviously best. The reason is pressure. To obtain a good impression, and an evenly inked print, of two pages each containing a type area of 3½ x 5½ inches (of, say, 12-point type) necessitates a very solid press carrying a chase measuring (inside) at least 10 by 8 inches.

This criterion is met by (a) old jobbing treadle presses of various makes, (b) very heavy hand platens, and (c) professional proof-presses in which the impression is supplied by a roller, not a platen. The lighter presses are excellent for jobbing work; but if used for bookwork will only print one page at a time, and probably only a forme measuring about 3 x 5 inches. At any rate, using such a machine, one's first book should be small; one can get more out of the machine later on. The Adana machine makes up to some extent for its lightness by its great speed and simplicity — it is quick to change from one page to the next, and the sheets can stick out of the machine without inking, in three directions. It is perfectly capable of producing small editions of poetry and prose in this manner. It is an ideal machine for printing miniature books (Plate 6, p 33).

If justifying lines and transferring them from composing stick to galley is the tricky part of letterpress composition, the preparation or 'make-ready' is often the trickiest part of machining. Getting the impression right by getting platen and bed exactly parallel is achieved by tightening or loosening the impression screws incorporated for that purpose in the bed or platen of the machine. The packing behind the top sheet must be correct also — enough to enable the type to dig slightly into the paper, but not to emboss it. These operations are not always easy when formes are uneven — a problem confined to letterpress. The owner of a letterpress machine must learn by experience, especially in the use of 'type-high' bearers. Small machines do press more heavily on isolated segments of type than on massed type. Then there is the problem of some areas proving weaker in impression even in massed type in pages. It may be because the type is worn. The impression must be built up by pasting tissue onto the top sheet. All the old manuals contain the fullest instructions on this matter. Fortunately, book production — runs of regular oblongs of type — do minimise the need for such 'make-ready'; often very little is needed with a heavy machine and nearly new type (Plate 34).

A book heavily inked on one page and lightly inked on its fellow page looks amateurish. The careful control of ink on the ink-plate is a small department of printing art, involving the regular addition of very small blobs of ink from a palette knife at intervals of 30 to 100 copies, depending on the machine.

Treadle presses are better than the hand-presses and ideal for printing two (even four) pages at a time, fast and evenly. We cannot here expatiate on the details of operating one, but there is no lack of manuals. We should add that, while letterpress printing is free of any health hazard, no treadle or powered machine should be operated without its hand-guard being fully operational. And if children are about, the flywheel should be fenced.

155

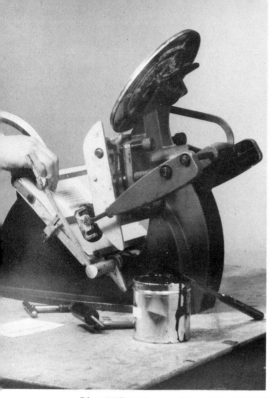

Plate 33 Printing machines: (*top left*) Adana, 8in x 5in printing area, a clam-action platen with automatic inking; (*top right*) a Model No 3 with 9in x 7in printing area, a clam-action platen with automatic inking; (*below*) a commercial proofing-press with power inking, paper register, flatbed for chase and printing area of 25in x 36in; (*opposite top*) a treadle-operated 'cropper' clam-action press with printing area 13in x 9in showing operator feeding paper (guard removed for clarity)

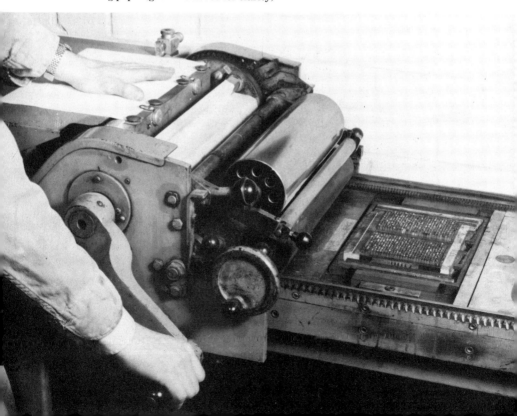

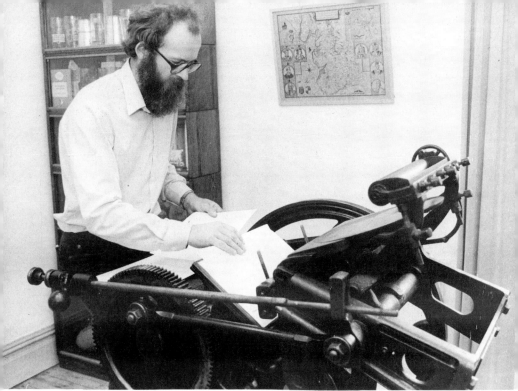

Plate 34 'Make-ready' of the packing on the platen of a platen press, seen from above. (*Left*) weak impression area located on top sheet and pricked, then (*left below*), a piece of tissue inserted at marked spot

Such machines are no longer manufactured. Second-hand, a machine with a chase measurement of 10 x 8 inches will cost from £180 to £300; a motorised machine costs up to £600 — but bargains occur. They weigh over 4cwt and need a solid floor.

Flatbed machines, in which the roller exerts the pressure, are available in the form of proof-presses. These are excellent for small editions if provided with lay gauges for accurate register. They can print eight standard-sized pages at a time, so only operators with substantial resources of type will find them worth while. They are splendid for printing wood engravings, half-tones, etc. They cost — when they can be found, which is rarely — about £600. They need a very solid floor.

A bench-mounted clam-action platen, regarded as movable without dismantling, costs second-hand £100 upwards and weighs up to 1cwt. Chase sizes do not exceed 11 x 8 inches.

When buying second-hand it is highly advisable to see the machine running with a fairly full forme. If the work it produces is good, it is unlikely to have serious faults. Not only are letterpress machines cheaper than small offset machines producing comparable work, but they are more robust and easier to maintain.

Letterpress and litho are alternatives, but are also complementary, as we have explained in Chapter 5.

Comparisons of approximate capital outlay on second-hand offset-litho equipment and letterpress equipment

Litho		Letterpress	
ORIGINATION	£		£
Typewriter, golf ball, manual, carbon		50lb type	50–250*
		Spaces and leads	10–30
ribbon	50–150	Reglet, furniture	10*
electric	100–250	4 steel galleys	6
Variable space		Composing stick	3–12
typewriter	200–900**		
Varityper	600–900**		
Composer, strike-on			
IBM type	1,300–4,500*		
Composer, electronic			
photosetter	1,500–5,000*		
IMPOSITION			
Design board/light		Quoins, 12	6
box	15–120	Chases, 4	25–40
Paste-up items	50	Minor tools	20
Packet plates	50	Lead-cutter/	
Platemaker	150–1,500*	shears	20
Process camera and			
components	200–2,000*		

Offset-litho machine, print area		Hand press, print area	
9½ x 13 in	300–600	5 x 8 in	100–250
		10 x 8 in	150–300
		Treadle, print area	
		11 x 13 in	160–600**
		Powered, print area	
		11 x 13 in	200–600**

(Recurrent costs, plates, chemicals, maintenance, ink not included — a major factor in litho)
* New   ** Reconditioned

10
ILLUSTRATIONS

Artists and illustrators

The many references to illustration in the preceding chapters will suggest that many, if not all, home publishers think in terms of illustrated books and periodicals. This is certainly the tradition of the private presses. In this chapter we shall mainly confine ourselves to practicalities, the methods by which, using both old and new technologies, home publishers can compete with commercial books in the use of illustration.

The first question that arises is, *who* is to *do* the illustrations, whether for books or periodicals. Many private-press owners are, of course, themselves artists, or are married to, or are teamed up with, artists. Some artists become publishers, as we mentioned in Chapter 2, to provide a medium for their art, or a way of publicising and distributing it. No problems arise; such artists and illustrators have only to exploit such opportunities as the new technologies offer to their particular genre of visual art.

Those with more modest talents, or who are developing their talents, may also find that they can tackle illustration with the aid of the new technologies. They need the private presses and independent publishers as much as the latter need them. Here we shall hastily bypass the hoary theme of the difference between artists and illustrators. Some artists look down on illustrators as an inferior class, just as they deprecate mere craftsmen, instead of distinguishing them solely by talent and merit.

Many of the greatest artists, ranging from Hans Holbein to Henri Toulouse-Lautrec have illustrated books and even posters. One could mention dozens. What matters to the home publisher is this: a first-rate artist with an established reputation, whose name on the title page will add lustre and sales appeal to his imprint, will be able to charge much more than an unestablished artist, whose merit awaits recognition.

It may seem a happy alternative to encourage the unestablished talent at a more modest outlay. Many private presses have done this, even helping to establish reputations. However the products of our art schools often expect to secure top fees for work of rather modest quality. They have been taught that they are 'exploited' by 'the system' and this in their eyes is apt to include the small publisher and printer. Commercial artists, as they are called, expect high fees because they are trained to do very specialised work for advertising and publicity firms who can afford to pay pretty well — but who dictate the specifications of the product. Commercial artists who are not obtaining a large flow of commissions, nonetheless fear to do work for a private press at a 'cut rate' lest knowledge of this should derogate from their status.

The world of art, illustration and commercial art is complicated, and we should be presumptuous to offer guidelines based on anything but our own limited experience. This is that artists must live and illustration tends to be expensive. One can only tell an artist what can be afforded and abide by the reaction. Something will depend on the reputation of the press. If an artist likes the press and its philosophy as well as its craftsmanship, he or she may accept what can be afforded simply for the fun of the thing, especially if there is a chance of experimenting with a new technique.

While a commercial artist is familiar with all the techniques of printing and will expect to supply his artwork to fit an agreed layout and method of reproduction, artists who only occasionally turn to illustration may not; nor is it advisable to try to dictate to them if one wishes to keep their name. They may produce work that requires to be commercially subcontracted because one has not oneself the capacity to print it. The best plan, in these circumstances, is to grin and bear it. Art is art.

This chapter will certainly not attempt any critique of the state of the art of illustration today, or offer any scale of costs of commissions. On the whole, the home publisher will be wise to avoid artists' agents when searching for illustrators. It is best to find them socially.

Finding illustrations

Copyright in artists' work is a complex legal matter, but if illustrations by someone else are to be reproduced, it is advisable to follow the guidelines — or call in advice. Usually artists own the copyright in their work, regardless of who actually possesses it, and this copyright continues for fifty years after death. However, when an artist makes an engraving, woodcut, linocut, etching or lithograph which has been *commissioned*, the copyright belongs to the commissioner. The copyright on old engravings in *Punch* or the *Illustrated London News* belongs to the proprietors of those magazines, and expires 50 years after the artist's death. The owner of the copyright can give or sell rights of reproduction to others, and most will do so for a small fee. The problem is often to find the owner.

There is a boom in 'clip art' — old illustrations, cuts and vignettes, etc,

WINDSOR GINGERBREAD

(a recipe published by Lyles Golden Syrup over 40 years ago)

1 lb flour
½ lb butter
½ lb raisins
3 eggs
1 teaspoon baking powder
½ teaspoon ground cinnamon
small teaspoon baking soda
1 cup Lyles Golden Syrup
½ lb caster sugar
2/3 cup mixed candied peel
½ cup sour cream
1 teaspoon ground ginger
½ teaspoon ground cloves
tablespoon boiling water

Cream butter and sugar. Heat syrup in saucepan. Beat in butter and sugar. Add well-beaten egg yolks and cream. Stir in soda dissolved in boiling water. Mix well. Stir in chopped raisins and peel. Stir in flour sifted with spice and baking powder. Lastly fold in the stiffly frothed egg whites. Beat. Bake in greased shallow baking tin in a slow oven for 2 hours.

A Lacre van used by Lyles c 1911

14

THE BREWHOUSE GALLERY: ETON COLLEGE

One may ask why Brewhouse? A reasonable question. The answer is because it was the building wherein the beer was brewed for College use. One may then ask why was the College, catering mainly for the education of boys, brewing beer? Beer in the 15th century and much later was an important item in the diet of the boys and staff and of most other people as well.

It is reasonable to assume that the founder, King Henry the Sixth, when he made his plans for building the College in 1440, would have included a brewhouse and bakehouse after the pattern of Winchester College. In David Loggan's engraving of the College, circa 1690, the brewhouse and bakehouse are shown and named (on display). What happened to the original building is not known. It must have been demolished before 1714 when the present one was erected. This building was in continuous use as a brewhouse until 1875 when a fire destroyed its interior. This brought to an end the brewing of beer. There is a poster in the gallery, dated 1881, advertising the sale of the brewing plant. It was the Choir School until 1966 when the School ceased to exist.

It had long been recognised by the College authorities that a building was required to exhibit for enjoyment and study and to store and preserve some of the College treasures. After considerable renovation the old brewhouse was opened as Brewhouse Gallery, by Lord Salisbury, in 1969.

Naturally most of the items on view deal with the

15

HORLEY CHURCH AND YE OLDE SIX-BELLS

Smallfield (about two miles) and after crossing the M23 turn right into Broadbridge Lane. After another mile turn right into Church Road and Burstow.

BURSTOW

Passing by the modern developments in Church Lane we shall come to a secluded corner to find the church, along with the rectory, the manor house, a Sunday school and a weatherboarded cottage. The church is usually locked, but the interested visitor may obtain the key from the rectory. It has a strange-looking tower and spire, built entirely of timber and supported on great corner posts and weatherboarded. There are four crude pinnacles on the tower, which 'leans inwards'.

After looking round this interesting corner of Burstow we can continue down Church Lane and back through Horley to join the Reigate Road (A217). The brook which we cross on this road just after passing the Black Horse at Hookwood is Spencer's Gill, a tributary of the Mole, and a couple of miles further on the road crosses the Mole itself at Sidlow Bridge. The somewhat isolated church stands on the right opposite a corner garage.

This is where we turn left into Ironbottoms on the south bank of the river and continue through the pleasant open country to turn into Deanoak Lane after about a mile. We shall shortly cross over Deanoak Brook, another tributary of the Mole, and then find our way to Leigh (pronounced 'Lye').

LEIGH

Just before reaching Leigh there is a little lane on the right leading to Swain's Farm, a restored 17th century house where Ben Jonson spent some time.

6

THE PLOUGH AT LEIGH

7

culled from old magazines and printed ready for clipping without a fee
— Messrs Dover Books are the impresarios here. Useful in some periodicals reproduced by offset-litho, they seem of scant interest to publishers
of small editions of books.

On the whole it is best to do one's own searches; but of course if an old
book cannot be defaced it is necessary to have an adequate camera and
lighting system to reproduce an old illustration; sometimes a photocopier gives a good enough image for reproduction. Old illustrations
have to be used, or abused, in an imaginative way to add appeal to a
book. The obvious application is in books on local history or topography.

'Line' and 'tone'

Illustrations can be reproduced at the same time as the text and by the
same process, or by a different process. The latter course means more
trouble and possibly more expense, but it may be necessary to reproduce
the illustration. There is little point in reproduction that results in a
muddy blot because the illustration and process do not agree with each
other.

For convenience the methods of reproduction will be described under
the different printing processes. Two technical terms need first to be
clarified.

A line illustration is one normally in black and white with no inter-
mediate tones — no greys. It is technically the simplest to reproduce.
The original copy is best in sharp black and white, but of course it can be
reproduced from red and white, or otherwise; however, some colours do
not come out on film, and this can mar or ruin the result. Red and brown
come out as black on film, pale blue, as we have noted, as white. Yellow
appears as grey, and yellow paper poses difficulties.

The printed result can be printed in any colour on any coloured paper.

A tone illustration is, by contrast, one in which there are shades of
grey, as occurs in a black and white photograph or a 'line and wash'
drawing. Such illustrations cannot be reproduced as they are. They are,
for reproduction, broken up into tiny dots which vary in size, large in
dark areas, small in light: these are half-tone illustrations; and the finer

(*opposite*) ——————————————————————————————
Plate 35 Two litho-printed local-history guides showing use of illustration in line
(reproduced here using screen), with typewritten text; (*top left, bottom picture*) a photograph reproduced as line, losing all grey shades (Shops Book, Neil Griffiths); (*top right*) a
typical line drawing; (*bottom*) showing use of line to create the effect of tone by (*left*)
adhesive tint patterns and (*right*) by fine shading lines by Don Goodacre

the pattern of dots the nearer the copy to the original. In some processes, line and tone are combined, the better to preserve the sharpness of the original.

Coloured illustrations can be either line or tone, single colour, multi-colour or full colour. A single colour picture will be either line or tone, merely printed in coloured ink, perhaps to blend better with the text; this is often known as a 'second colour' job. Multicoloured work means printing several matching pictures on top of each other in different coloured (and semi-transparent) inks — obviously an increasingly complex procedure as the number of colours is multiplied, or the detail grows. The home printer can easily manage two colours, but needs to master the art of exact register if he goes on to three or more.

Full-colour work, such as reproducing full-colour photographs, or an artist's picture in full colour, is a specialised process requiring photographic and printing skills acquired only after training. Large machines are normally used. It is very common in commercial work but has little relevance to home production. A page reproduced in full colour for insertion in a home-printed book can be bought out, but a charge of £200 for 1,000 copies of a single side of an A4-sized sheet would be typical. This might be considered for a cover regularly used for a magazine with the issue number and date overprinted, but otherwise it seems beyond the scope of this book. Ordinary photographic copies, pasted in, are cheapest for small amounts, and there are new photo-copying methods such as Xerox and Copyrun for larger numbers — but they are aimed at business users rather than printers, and will be located under business services in directories.

Illustrations for letterpress

These are all in relief, like type itself, and must consist of a level surface at type height with the non-printing areas cut away. Because the method of printing is direct, the illustration is mirror-image on the printing surface. The surface can be prepared by hand or photographically, the cutting away by hand or chemically. They are illustrated opposite.

Linocutting is the simplest method and the best-known. The technique is described in many art books and need not be repeated here. It is suitable for young artists in school; yet famous artists have used it to achieve certain broad effects, so it is not to be despised. It is simple and cheap, but to be effective it calls for talent. The softness of lino prevents fine lines, and the pressure of printing may distort the detail.

Plate 36 Blocks and plates, mounted and unmounted, for letterpress printing of illustrations. From top left: wood engraving, woodcut, linocut lettering for title page, half-tone of photograph, Victorian wood engraving, line block, linocut initial letter, line plate of a tailpiece, line block from a photograph, line block for a line drawing, unmounted photopolymer plate, unmounted linocut, unmounted zinco

Plate 37 Mounting materials for letterpress plates (to bring them type-high): chipboard, metal mounts, mounting board, wood mounting quads in em sizes, and a plate-lifting tool

Fig 31 Prints of some of the blocks shown in Plate 36

Wood engraving is a similar process of cutting away the non-printing areas; the hardness of the wood, normally 'end-grain', calls for training and skill; and special gravers and tools are needed, whereas passable linocuts can be made with a simple knife. Sharp detail is possible, and the results are generally considered most 'in sympathy' with letterpress printing. The two have been combined for some 500 years of fine book production and illustration.

Wood cuts historically precede wood engravings, but the effect must be broader since the side of the wood is used. They are cheaper, especially for large areas, as wood for engraving such large areas must be made up of small pieces dovetailed together (and often several engravers used to collaborate on such a picture made in several sections).

All three methods give line illustrations; they are often used for illustration with considerable areas of flat colour; but this can pose

166

difficulties within both the inking and pressure capacities of the press. As a rule-of-thumb, a letterpress platen machine will only cope with an average block a quarter of the printing area in size; cylinder printing machines, like the proofing press shown in Plate 33, printing only a small strip at a time, can cope with larger wood or lino blocks. Inking for platens is less of a problem, as it is often possible to ink the block twice for each impression to ensure an even and complete layer of ink. However, when type and blocks are together, this will result in over-inking of the type, so the two are often more conveniently printed separately, and then there is an incentive to print them attractively in a contrasting colour, lending richness to the appearance of a page. Make-ready (see pp 154–5) is used to ensure even pressure over blocks and type, the blocks usually needing extra packing to achieve the required pressure, and this complication is another disadvantage of printing both at once.

The costs are small: 10cm square will cost a few pence for lino, perhaps £5 for prepared wood — a little more if either are mounted type high. No time can be given: an artist may take two hours or a week to produce a wood engraving.

Photo-engraved plates are metal sheets of copper, zinc or magnesium, coated with photographic lacquer, and etched with acid to produce the required image in relief. They can be line illustrations or half-tones.

The major piece of equipment required, a process camera (see Fig 24) is used for the first step. The illustration to be reproduced is photographed on to special 'lith' film and enlarged or reduced at the same time to the required size. A new camera, capable of illustrations up to A3 size, will cost from £1,000 upwards; a second-hand one from about £200.

The operation is similar to that for making litho plates described in Chapter 7. The film is laid onto the metal sheet with its special lacquer, and exposed to ultra-violet light for a minute or two; the light shining through the film hardens the lacquer. The plate so treated is washed, removing unhardened lacquer, and dipped or sprayed in acid (usually nitric) which etches away the unwanted areas. This etching process requires a special machine, because the acid must not eat away under the edges of the image but leave a supporting bank. The machines use an oil to do this. It is possible to achieve the same result by hand etching, using a powder called dragon's blood to protect the edges, but it is a slow, tricky process and we know few amateurs who can use this process.

To make half-tones, a screen of dots is used at the photographing stage to produce the appropriate sizes of dots on the negative and plate (see page 163 above). After etching, excess metal is cut away and the block mounted. Mounting is expensive and those who buy blocks can save money by mounting them on special mounting blocks of the correct

167

height, secured by double-sided tape or other adhesive (see Plate 36).

This process, described in detail in technical books, is used by 'process engravers' so listed in trade directories. They offer a fast service with orders despatched on day of receipt, and a choice of metals (copper is dearer and not needed for short runs) as well as other services, like cutting holes in the plate for inserting type. The price charged depends on the type of illustration (line, 'fine line with great detail', or half-tone), the area and any extras such as mounting. The minimum price in 1983 was about £7 for line blocks and £9 for half-tones of 10sq cm. When ordering, it is necessary to specify the final size required (either in terms of the bottom line or the proportional increase or decrease), and, in the case of half-tone, the screen, or number of dots per square inch. Rough papers need 85 screen, 100 screen is for smooth papers, while 133 screen can only be printed effectively on 'art' paper. If a sample of the paper is sent, the engraver will advise what is best. Those using process engravers' services are advised to study technical manuals on this subject for background information and ideas for special usages.

Half-tones require considerable printing pressure so that the area that can be printed on a platen is severely limited, especially as half-tones are often printed with text, since this presents few inking problems. The original photographs or artwork also need consideration as the half-tone process reduces detail and contrast.

Polymer plates are a recent innovation. They are similar to photo-engraved ones, but the plate itself is a light-sensitive plastic coated on a thin but tough metal backing sheet. The procedure is otherwise the same as for other plates, but instead of etching with acid, the plate is scrubbed gently in a bath of warm methylated spirits to remove the unwanted areas. Provided precautions are taken against fire and fumes, this is an easy process to do at home.

It requires a process camera as described above, but even this can be dispensed with if one works from hand-drawn negatives: ie the artist paints with photographic opaque paint on a clear plastic sheet, painting the areas *not* wanted. The only special materials to be purchased are the actual plates, supplied in packets of 25 sheets of usually A4 size at £60 per pack. Plates have a limited shelf life of about a year.

Photopolymer plates are thin, so the engraving of the non-printing areas is shallow, and there is a danger of the blank parts being inked by rollers set too low, and marking the paper under platen pressure. The answer is to cut away the unwanted parts and adjust both rollers and platen pressure — and the platen packing. It is sometimes possible to use a 'frisket' (cut-out mask) to protect the blank areas from contact with the block; it was a common procedure in the old printing craft.

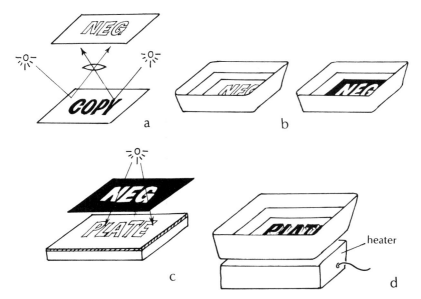

a   b

c   heater   d

Fig 32 The stages in making a photopolymer plate: (a) making negative in process camera; (b) developing negative; (c) exposing plate through negative to ultra-violet light (held in contact, preferably in a vacuum back); (d) scrubbing in bath of warm methylated spirits

Illustrations for litho

We have already pointed out that offset-litho has greatly eased the problem of illustration — the illustrations can simply be pasted in as part of the artwork.

However, this is not possible with tone illustrations which must be converted into half-tones, necessitating recourse to the process camera and a screen to make a half-tone negative; this in turn being printed photographically to give a half-tone paper print.

With CT or electrostatic plates (p 119), this can be fixed into the artwork and a plate made in the usual way. It could also be done this way with pre-sensitised plates; but it gives better results to photograph the rest of the artwork and then cut a hole in that negative to fix in ('strip in') the negative of the half-tone (Fig 25). Such considerations strengthen the case for investing in a process camera: it permits the best use of the best platemaking method, and allows the camera adept to play other tricks with the artwork, enlarging or reducing items, repeatedly copying them in fine detail and reversing black for white or right for left, which may enliven the appearance of periodicals or community newspapers. It is less significant for small editions.

Direct-image litho plates permit the most elementary means of illustration or ornamentation — drawing or painting straight onto the plate itself.

169

Other methods of illustrating

Litho and relief printing are not the only methods of reproduction. Other methods are worth considering, depending on circumstances and facilities available. Each form of replication has its own method and feel, and will make its own contribution to the atmosphere of the work.

Duplicating can reproduce simple line illustrations quite well, though the fuzziness added by the process must be taken into account. It can only be used, of course, on the absorbent papers integral to the process. There are three ways of producing the stencil.

Ordinary stencils (as used for typing texts) can be 'cut' by hand with a stylus. This is available from office supply and art materials shops, and is preferable to the use of a ballpoint. Special aids are available from duplicating machine manufacturers such as tooth wheels to make dotted lines and pattern plates to place behind the stencil for rubbing areas of pattern or shading. The aim throughout is to push the wax coating aside enough to allow the ink to be squeezed through without tearing the soft gauzelike backing support. The method can only be recommended to publishers of news-sheets severely stretched for cash!

Thermal or electronic stencil makers are better. The former makes a stencil by a photocopying process, but is not always easy to control and it can 'see' as black materials those which the human eye sees as white, notably typists' correcting fluid. The electronic method 'scans' the artwork, cutting a stencil with a spark, and it can reproduce photographs tolerably well (not as well as litho) and is much used by estate agents for handouts. Maladjusted, it renders the scanning lines noticeable and the lettering is fuzzier than on directly typed stencils. These stencils are made commercially by local typing service firms for £1–£2 each; or alternatively the machines can be bought second-hand for £50 upwards. The specialised stencils cost around 10–12p.

Screen process printing strictly includes duplicating but is more recognisable as the process which will probably have been encountered at school as 'silk screen'. Simple as it is, it can achieve highly sophisticated results in skilled hands. It is fully covered in instruction manuals, and only a few notes will be appended here (see Fig 33).

The requirements are a wooden frame with a gauze to stretch over it, a squeegee (wooden handle with a rubber blade) and suitable ink — all available from artists' suppliers. Stencils can be made by hand by cutting paper or painting directly on the gauze, and printing requires only a flat surface and space to dry prints. Speed is about 100 copies an hour, so this process is well suited to short runs and small editions.

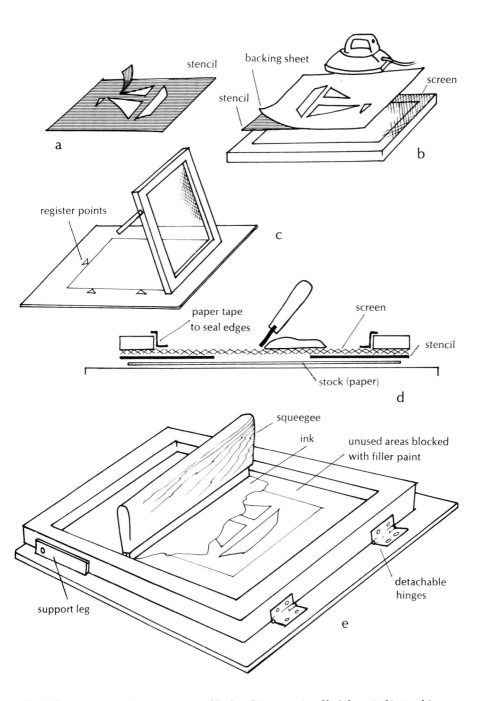

Fig 33 Screen process: (a) cutting stencil by hand (paper or 'profilm' sheets); (b) attaching stencil to screen ('profilm' is attached by heat, paper can be glued on); (c) the screen attached to baseboard; (d) side view of screen; (e) making a print

171

For more sophisticated requirements there is the photographic method of exposing the screen to ultra-violet light; though to fully exploit the potential of the method a process camera is needed to make negatives (page 122). The coated screen or the film is exposed to the light through a positive or negative, depending on the chemical used, and when washed or developed, emerges as a stencil. It is cheap, costing perhaps one pound per screen, and there are specialist suppliers who will make screens from customers' artwork.

Screen printing lays down a relatively thick layer of ink compared to other methods. It is useful in particular situations, such as in printing white on top of dark colours, printing on cloth or wood, and to give a vivid impact. Large areas are no great problem, nor are solid areas. Though best for such effects it *can* be used for detail in practised hands.

Artwork is the same as for other methods and is normally line only — photographs come out as very coarse half-tones. It is rarely used commercially in books, but is a real possibility for colour illustrations in small editions. Above all, it is excellently suited to produce covers in bright colours with informal lettering, and is worth mastering as a genuine solution to the cover problems discussed in this book. It complements small letterpress, each being best where the other has limitations, and it requires little capital or permanent space.

Etching and engraving are traditional techniques, excellent for book illustration and widely used before the advent of photography and litho. They are now normally too expensive for commercial publishers. They require the highest skills and a special press which is expensive; this is a method for a home publisher based on, or teamed with, an art school.

Twopence coloured

Let us repeat that nothing so enhances a small edition as the use of illustration and colour. It is perhaps worth remarking that if a book is illustrated by pictures in line, it is not impossible, using a stencil or other guidelines, to add colour with a simple paintbrush dipped in watercolour or poster colour ink. This was the method practised for embellishing the woodcuts of the chapbooks and street ballads of the eighteenth and nineteenth centuries. Jeremy Catnach, the leader in this field, kept his wife and daughters hard at it in a back room colouring the ballads he printed in the front room at Seven Dials. It doubled the price, as is well known. (We are told that such a division of labour is occasionally practised by some contemporary private presses.) The fact remains that the phrase 'hand-coloured' inflates the price of books in second-hand dealers' catalogues.

11
PAPER, INK, CONCLUSIONS

Basic paper policy

Paper is a subject as wide as printing; we have made some references to it, and we can now only set out what seems to be of most importance to the home publisher. We find that it is a difficult problem for many amateur printers, too many of whom accept without question the paper their local printers or paper merchants offer them. Too many assume that provided the design of the book is right and the typography acceptable, the cheapest paper will do.

This may be right for the spare-time jobbing printer; it may also be right for the periodical publisher who has to think of his postal costs; it is totally wrong for the maker of small editions. Their whole point is that they are hand-crafted semi-luxury products, and quality must run right through them. Because the cost of paper *looks* a relatively large item in the out-of-pocket costs of printing, there is a tendency to think economies should be made here.

In reality the publisher is processing and re-selling paper at a high price ratio. Consequently the price of this basic raw material is a minor item in the final selling price. But it is a major factor in the sales appeal of the product itself. To halve the cost of the paper makes little difference to the net price that small editions, produced along the lines we have been discussing, can command. It may, however, make the book itself seem shoddy. Oddly enough, it is often not the design or typography of a book that appeals to the buyer of 'something different'. It is the feel of the paper itself; this is what makes the book look rich and rare and special.

The extreme case is hand-made books printed on hand-made paper. Such paper, English or imported, costs about four times as much as the best machine-made paper, five times as much as an average book paper. Yet printing on it allows a private press to sell at six times a comparable edition on machine-made paper; buyers (mostly collectors) will pay £10 to £15 for the hand-made paper edition, against an 'ordinary' edition of, say, £2.50. Of course these prices imply fine printing by letterpress. Some private press books would not sell at all unless printed on hand-made paper. There are now some strictly commercial outfits printing undistinguished books in fancy but mass-made bindings on hand-made paper, because they can make profits thereby. The *ne plus ultra* of the situation occurs when the home publisher prints on his own home-hand-made paper.

Machine-made paper comes in great variety and it is sound policy to hunt around for good qualities. The object of this chapter is not to cover the vast and intricate field of the paper trade, but to offer suggestions on how to get at the right paper for the edition.

Ink

Here we will just interpolate the point that it is important to use a good quality ink on a good quality paper. They reinforce each other. Ink warrants a little thought and trouble. The printing machines, whether small offset or letterpress, available to home printers have limited rolling powers and one must therefore buy fully finished, high quality inks, of which the best are the commercial proofing inks. This means paying more, but the difference between using good ink and 'jobbing' ink is small.

Litho and letterpress inks differ. It is possible to use litho ink for letterpress but not the other way about. Litho ink also deteriorates faster in the can than letterpress ink, which is almost everlasting and is also about 30 per cent cheaper. Ault & Wiborg and Shackell Edwards make good litho inks, and the letterpress ranges still available from Winstone & Co, and Shuck Maclean & Co, are reliable.

Black ink is straightforward if applied correctly — that is, starting with too little and gradually adding to it. Printing in colour, important to the small edition publisher, needs great care. A wide range of ready-made coloured inks exist; the shade can be tested by touching it lightly with the finger and dabbing it on white paper. One often needs more transparency. This is achieved by stocking a tin of what is called 'tinting medium', which behaves like ink but is colourless; to it coloured ink can be added to the shade desired. From a stock of red, blue, yellow, green, brown and above all *white* ink, one can mix colours as from an artist's palette. White ink, added to other colours, permits the printing of a lighter shade on a darker background, such as a cover board. Driers should also be stocked; added to ink they hasten drying, important when printing on smooth and especially 'art' paper (see below) to avoid 'set off'.

The paper revolution

The advent of offset-litho and mass production of books has greatly changed both the techniques of making paper and the range on offer.

The offset machine, in any of its sizes, performs best on a smooth, hard paper. Letterpress looks best on a softer paper, or a paper with a yielding core, so that the type can bite into it without embossing it. (Of old, and with hand-made paper, paper was printed damp.) Today the decline of letterpress means that hard papers are in the ascendant, and grades that are 'kind to letterpress' take a little finding.

Paper varies in *weight* and *thickness*, which are nearly reciprocals of each other; in *surface finish*, ranging from rough and hairy to glassy smooth; and in *colour*, from 'high whites' to 'deep creams'. These variations in the quality of paper derive from its ingredients and treatment in manufacture.

To summarise: these ingredients are mostly 'boiled tree' or 'minced tree' (technically, chemical wood or mechanical wood), sometimes with an addition of esparto grass, sometimes with a proportion of re-cycled (within the mill) paper, or even de-inked re-cycled wastepaper. White mineral fillers — china clays — close the pores and a binder — size — helps glue the felted structure together. Paper has a grain: if possible it should only be creased and folded with the grain — especially with covers — which can be found by seeing how easily it tears in either direction, or inspection of the torn edge. The rule is : easy tear = with the grain; hard tear = across the grain. In addition, paper stretches more across the grain than along it when affected by damp (eg when printing by litho). This can cause problems of registration when printing in two or more colours, and especially in precision work such as four-colour process (see p 164). If care is taken to keep paper at an even temperature and humidity, no real problems occur in the normal small job with small-sized sheets.

Surface, weight, thickness

Surface — Any layman knows some papers are shiny, others are roughish. The shiny is generically known as 'art', and gets an extra coating of clay which is polished smooth between steel rollers; it is used for half-tones of 100 screen and over. Thin art papers should be avoided by amateurs.

Next come the 'blade coated cartridge' papers, which are standard for litho. Slightly less smooth are the 'twin wire cartridges' which are actually two sheets of paper joined back to back to give identical sides: they provide the highest quality litho reproduction. Tullis Russell Ltd, makers of Mellotex, are leaders in this paper.

Less smooth are the uncoated cartridge papers, suitable in the heavier grades for letterpress, because they have that softer core that is 'kind to type'.

Finally come the imitation 'laid papers' with the pronounced ribbed finish that gives a pleasant old-world feel to books; they are generically known as 'antique laids'.

Some possibilities may be set out as follows:

For offset-litho	For letterpress
Huntsman Superwhite	Basingwerk Parchment
Mellotex	Basingwerk Book Art
Ivorex	Longbow
High Speed Blade	Conqueror Laid
Chariot Cartridge	Inverurie Cartridge
Clan Book Wove	Glastonbury Antique Laid

It is wise to avoid papers with chemical or fluorescent whiteners, especially for colour printing.

Weight Paper is graded in terms of metric grams per square metre of a single sheet: gsm or g/m^2, terms we have earlier introduced. Formerly, weight was expressed in lbs per ream of 500 sheets of a given sheet area, or 'broadside'; the Americans still do.

Paper can be thin but heavy, like banknotes, or thick but puffy like the 'featherweight antique' often used for children's annuals. The reason is density. We suggest that the small edition needs a paper that is heavy but not too dense, if it is to be deliberately bulked up for thickness in binding. To find such paper, the publisher should discuss his needs with a good paper merchant.

Weight can be tested by the fingers; it is surprising how sensitive to differences of two-thousandths of an inch our fingers can become! Visually and tactually this means that office copy paper is about 60gsm, a goodish 'bond' writing paper about 85gsm. Paperbacks are often printed on 70gsm near-newsprint, but a book of good quality on 120gsm 'antique laid'. We feel a small edition book calls for at least 120gsm 'antique laid' or similar.

Paper sizes

Most standard paper is now stocked in sizes related to sub-divisions of a master sheet with the area of a square metre. These are the A sizes referred to in previous chapters. The master sheet 'A0' measures 841mm x 1189mm which in fact is an area of a square metre. The sub-divisions of this (largely theoretical) master sheet are called 'the A sizes' and are as follows (with approximate inch equivalents):

A0	841 x 1189mm	33.1 x 46.8 inches
A1 (one fold)	594 x 841mm	23.4 x 33.1 inches
A2 (two folds)	420 x 594mm	16.5 x 23.4 inches

A3 (three folds)	297 x 420mm	11.7 x 16.5 inches
A4 (four folds)	210 x 297mm	8.3 x 11.7 inches
A5 (five folds)	148 x 210mm	5.8 x 8.3 inches

Fig 34 shows these subdivisions. A standard page size is now often 'A5', which means that to print four pages on a sheet (two pages on each side) one buys the familiar 'A4' size. To print eight pages, four per side, one needs 'A3'.

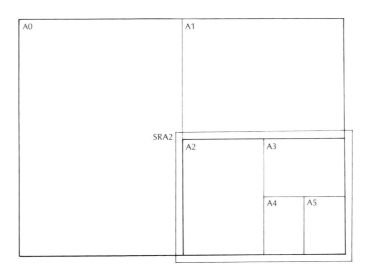

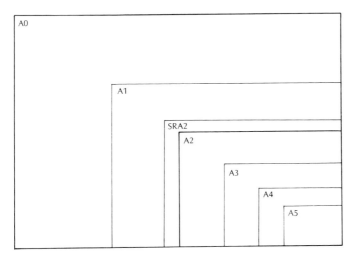

Fig 34 (a) the international or DIN sizes of paper, showing how A0 subdivides, and one 'SRA' size for comparison (the sheets all extend to bottom right-hand corner); (b) the same sizes rearranged to show their identical proportions

This standardisation is hailed as a great advance and its convenience is self-evident. But it is better adapted to office stationery than to true bookwork. The A5 shape is not particularly sympathetic to true typography (though it *is* suitable to the wide typefaces of typewriters and ragged right margins as already noted). In addition there is the question of an allowance for holding the edges of the paper by the gripper-fingers of big machines, and for trimming the finished book by guillotine.

To meet this, the A0 sizes have been adjusted, and now if one buys paper from printers or substantial paper merchants *for printing,* one is likely to be offered the slightly larger RA and SRA sizes. The difference, however, is only a few millimetres. Thus the RA0 master sheet is 860 x

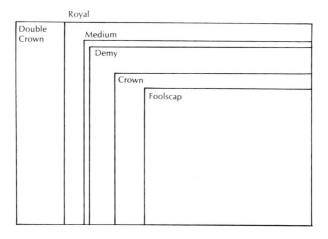

Fig 35 (a) a family of related 'old sizes' of paper based on a 'crown sheet'; (b) the common imperial or 'old' sizes still in use

178

1220mm against the A0 sheet of 841 x 1189mm, while the SRA0 sheet is 900 x 1280mm. So RA3 sheets are 305 x 430mm, and SRA3 sheets are 320 x 450mm, compared with A3, 297 x 420mm. It is only necessary to know what one is buying.

Parallel with these standard metric sizes some of the 'old sizes' persist. Centuries of experience, good taste, and the exigencies of the old hand presses evolved the old sizes. When folded into book-sized pages they produce a variety of elegant 'portrait' shapes, comely to the eye, good for well-proportioned line measures, and therefore conducive to easy reading. The A sizes, valuable for commercial printing because they fit standard envelopes, etc, cannot match the convenience of the old sizes in book design. The old sizes that are still on offer, measured in inches with metric equivalents (see Fig 35), are:

	Broadside (sheet)	Folio (folded once)	Quarto (folded twice)	Octavo (folded thrice)
Royal	20 x 25	12½ x 20	10 x 12½	6¼ x 10
	508 x 635	*318 x 508*	*254 x 318*	*159 x 254*
Double Crown	20 x 30	15 x 20	10 x 15	7½ x 10
	508 x 762	*381 x 508*	*254 x 381*	*191 x 254*
Double medium	23 x 36	18 x 23	11½ x 18	9 x 11½
	457 x 584	*292 x 457*	*229 x 292*	*146 x 229*
Double demy	22½ x 35	17½ x 22½	11¼ x 17½	8¾ x 11¼
	572 x 890	*445 x 572*	*286 x 445*	*222 x 286*
Medium	18 x 23	11½ x 18	9 x 11½	5¾ x 9
	457 x 584	*292 x 457*	*229 x 292*	*146 x 229*
Demy	17½ x 22½	11¼ x 17½	8¾ x 11¼	5⅝ x 8¾
	445 x 572	*286 x 445*	*222 x 286*	*143 x 222*
Large Post	16½ x 21	10½ x 16½	8¼ x 10½	5¼ x 8¼
	419 x 533	*267 x 419*	*210 x 267*	*133 x 210*

('Old' sizes in inches, metric equivalents in millimetres)

Hand-made and mould-made papers

Hand-made paper is usually sold by the sheet and in one of the old sizes, rather than by weight. It is no longer made by pounded and cleaned rags, but from 'virgin' cotton fibre which makes it a little harder. There are various surfaces, ranging from 'Hot press', the smoothest, to 'Rough' and 'Not' which are very rough. There are degrees of sizing. Hand-mades are often unsuitable for small offset or photocopying, and must generally be damped before printing on letterpress machines. A lightly sized hand-made paper, may, in a damp period, pick up enough moisture from the atmosphere, but the stacks should not exceed 10–20 sheets to do so. There are several ways of damping. One way we have found suitable is to stack up to 50 sheets on a smooth surface — wood or glass —

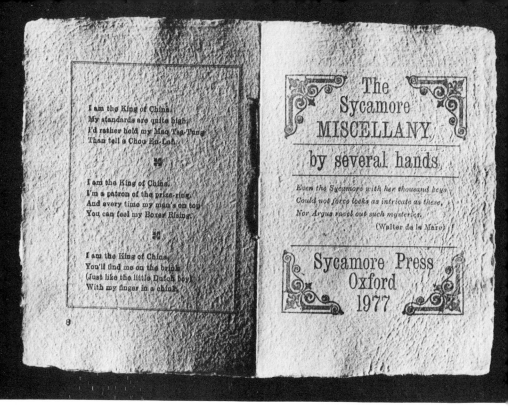

I am the King of China,
My standards are quite high;
I'd rather hold my Mao Tse-Tung
Than tell a Chou En-Lah.

I am the King of China,
I'm a patron of the prize-ring,
And every time my man's on top
You can feel my Boxer Rising.

I am the King of China,
You'll find me on the brink
(Just like the little Dutch boy)
With my finger in a chink.

The
Sycamore
MISCELLANY
by several hands

Even the Sycamore with her thousand keys
Could not force locks as intricate as these,
Nor Argus ravel out such mysteries.
(Walter de la Mare)

Sycamore Press
Oxford
1977

Plate 38 Total home production by John Fuller (Sycamore Press): a booklet printed by letterpress at home on home-made paper

with a sheet of damp blotting-paper between every 8–10 sheets. In two days the stack will absorb the moisture from the blotting-paper; some printers then put in freshly damped blotting-paper and reverse the stacks for two more days.

Some currently available brand names of hand-made and mould-made papers are — *English*: New Whatman, St Cuthbert's ranges (Somerset and Bockingford), J. Barcham Green, Sheepstor, and Heritage from Atlantis Paper Co. *German*: Zerkall. *Dutch*: Van Gelders (which *will* take litho). *French*: Canson's *mi-tientes* range. *Swedish*: Tre Kronor. *Italian*: Fabriano. Japanese hand-made is very thin and usually printed only on one side. The best way to study these papers is to visit the central London store of Falkiner Fine Papers in Long Acre, WC2, or Messrs Wiggins Teape, next door. They will often give advice.

Supplies

It is not necessary, however simple, to take what the local printer offers, or even what the local paper merchant offers. In any fair-sized town the 'Yellow Pages' will have addresses of several paper merchants and at least one is sure to accept small orders. They will mostly offer standard paper of under 100gsm, but one or two are likely to stock, or be ready to procure, a ream (500 sheets) of better quality paper. They will prefer to sell it by the 'packet', 'unbroken', in probably SRA2 size. Unless the publisher/printer has a fairly large guillotine he will want it cut to a smaller size. The normal charge for this is £2 per cut, and if he wants only half a ream, there will be a 'breaking charge' of £3 or £4. These charges reinforce the case for owning a guillotine and being able to cut one's own paper. It is very worth while so to plan one's paper needs that one can buy in reams of good quality paper instead of odd lots of poorer paper costing just as much when extra charges are added in. It is handy to have two thicknesses on hand, a 135/150gsm paper for booklets of 16–24 pages, and 120gsm for booklets of 32, 48 and more pages.

Paper mills do not sell direct to customers, but through merchants. Large commercial publishers buy large tonnages direct from mills made to their specification as to weight, quality and size. There are inevitably left-overs, broken reams and oddments which are often supplied to the so-called 'clearance houses' such as the Terrier Paper Co of Northampton, Harveys of Edinburgh and the Capital Paper Co of London. They issue weekly lists of what they have available and normally supply at well below mill prices. They also pick up odd lots — so-called 'trickles' — which they will let go really cheaply to a caller with his own transport; this is the best, even if troublesome, way to pick up really fine paper cheaply. For the small buyer there are also firms dealing with small orders by mail, such as Gemini Supplies Ltd of Shrewsbury.

Cover boards

Cover boards come in varieties too great to itemise, and we cannot here do more than repeat our advice to write to merchants for swatches of samples which are made up for this very reason (see pp 104–105). Cover papers (150gsm and over) are often sold by the half ream, and cover boards (over 250gsm) per hundred sheets (often in old sizes). The odd lots available from clearance houses are worth investigating. One should always be on the lookout for attractive cover papers or boards to be stored for future use.

Paper is sensitive to moisture and should be stored in a cool dry place in a wrapper, flat. Paper left in a pile with the edges exposed to dampness or dryness will develop wavy edges due to expansion or contraction of the edges. Boards and paper may discolour if the edges are exposed to sunlight.

Paperwork

We may conclude this book by tacking on to this chapter some final words on paper*work*, or 'admin'. The pleasure of home publishing and printing is that it carries no obligation to keep elaborate records or accounts or to bother with *admin*. When that develops, the press is verging on 'going commercial'; when Nancy Cunard found that the success of her Hours Press was leading in that direction, she promptly closed it down.

However, we find that a minimum of record-keeping is not too onerous. One needs invoices with printed headings to send out if one gets orders from customers; further, to approach printers, paper merchants etc, one needs printed letterheads and invoices to indicate the press is truly in business (otherwise they will not deliver by van, for instance). One needs a ring-binder or other file to preserve the copies, and a second one to keep receipted invoices in. A separate bank account for the press will, in juxtaposition with the contents of the ring-binders, show where one stands financially, especially if one keeps records of the outgoings on materials and maintenance. For an output of three books a year, this will be sufficient. It will not be sufficient (see p 140) for a periodical of any pretensions.

If the press is actually making money, the taxman will want his share, and accounts will have to be presented to him. But, in turn, the publisher is entitled to charge against any such profits, the depreciation of his equipment, expenses of running an office, travelling, and an agreed proportion of his house and home overheads. It is best to talk in friendly fashion with the Inspector if things come to this pass, and it becomes evident that one is actually getting into business. If the enterprise is then allowed to become a flourishing small business house, and we know a dozen that have, it may well become necessary to bring in accountants. At that prospect however, we prefer to bow out.

APPENDIX
INFORMATION AND SUPPLIES

Societies

The Association of Little Presses, 89A Petherton Road, London N5. A loose association of several hundred small publishers, with an approximately bi-monthly news-letter which keeps members informed of useful publishing information, bookshops and book fairs. Publishes useful booklets of advice mainly for authors and community presses, and issues an annual list of publications.

The British Printing Society, BM/ISPA, London WC1. Brings together people interested in all aspects and kinds of printing, from hobby to commercial, and publishes a monthly magazine *Small Printer*, issued free to members, containing articles on printing, advice, technical tips etc, on both litho and letterpress printing. There are regional branches where members meet regularly at each other's houses to discuss problems, compare techniques and buy and sell items. The majority of members are interested in making jobbing printing pay, but many members are small publishers in many fields. A useful contact for technical advice.

Federation of Alternative Booksellers, c/o Mushroom, 10 Heathcote Street, Nottingham NG1 3AA. This body loosely co-ordinates the interests of about fifty radical bookshops throughout the country, and may provide helpful information for small and very small publishers who produce left-wing oriented books.

Inter-Action, 15 Wilkin Street, London NW5 3NG. A group of trusts formed to stimulate community development with a publishing unit, Inprint, which issues practical guides, and a community printshop and media service.

The Private Libraries Association, 'Ravelston', South View Road, Pinner, Middlesex. Though essentially an association of bok collectors, it takes a special interest in private-press operations and in its quarterly journal *The Private Library* reviews private-press books and occasionally the work of individual presses. It also publishes annually Private Press Books with a listing of titles worldwide.

Equipment

General Many firms dealing in printing requirements can be found by consulting the 'Yellow Pages', under such headings as Bookbinding, Lithography, Printers, Printers' Services, Printers' Engineers, Printing Ink Manufacturers, Printing Plates, Process Engravers, Paper Merchants, Typesetters (this includes hot metal, IBM composition and phototypesetting), Typewriter Dealers.

Exchange and Mart has sections dealing with second-hand printing equipment of all kinds(including Varitypers). *Printing Trades Directory* covers commercial printers' second-hand equipment and auctions thereof.

Suppliers of type and printing accessories Some suppliers specialise in small quantities, often at higher prices. Large suppliers may impose a minimum charge making small orders impractical.

Adana Printing Machines, Church Street, Twickenham, Middlesex. (Machines, type, accessories, paper.)

Excelsior Printers Supply Co, City Gate Unit, Nobel Road, London N18. (Accessories, ink, second-hand machines.)

Merrion Foundries, 16 Groveway, London SW9 0AR. (Type, trade typesetting in Monotype faces, parlour presses.)

Mouldtype Ltd, Farringdon Road, London EC2, and North Road, Preston. (Type and accessories.)

Norfolk Printers, Norfolk Road, Sheringham, Norfolk. (Type.)

Startype, Horsfall and Sons, Birstall, Leeds. (Type and accessories.)

Stephenson Blake & Co, Sheaf Works, Maltravers Street, Sheffield. (Type, photosetting equipment, accessories.)

Caxtonia Ltd, 5 Pomeroy Drive, Industrial Estate, Oadby, Leics. (Paper and sundries.)

Selectasine Serigraphics, 65 Chislehurst Road, Chislehurst, Kent. (Screen process art equipment and accessories.)

Paper

Paper Facts and Figures magazine lists all brands and sizes available monthly, with stockists, but is only sold by annual subscription.

Gemini Paper Supplies, Unit 93, Condover Industrial Estate, Shrewsbury, Shropshire. Cut sizes of paper and board, and ink, by mail order.

Peter Gilbert Papers Ltd, 38 High Street, Milton-u-Wychwood, Oxfordshire.

Mastercraft Papers, Paper Mews, Dorking, Surrey.

Paper Sprint, Eastleigh, Hants.

(See Chapter 11 for other suppliers' names.)

Publishing Consultants

Coracle Press, 233 Camberwell New Road, London SE5.

Peter Stockham, 16 Cecil Court, London WC2N 4HE. -

Tony Ward, Arc & Throstle Press, Old Fire Station, Todmorden, Lancashire.

BIBLIOGRAPHY

Books, Bookshops and Bookselling

Babbage, B. *Beginning in Bookselling* (Grafton Press, 1975)
Baker, J. *The Book Business* (John Baker Publishers, 1971)
Booksellers Association *List of Members* (Annual)
Bundy, L. W. *Miniature Books* (Sheppard Press, 1981)
Cain, M. S. *Book Marketing* (Dustbooks, 1982)
Clique, The. *Directory of Booksellers* (Annual)
Hasselstrom, B. *The Book Book for Beginners* (Dustbooks, 1982)
Jennet, S. *The Making of Books* (Faber, 1963)
Margan, P. *Directory of Specialist Booksellers* (1983)
Myers, R. *British Book Trade* (Grafton, 1975)
Sheppard Press (ed). *European Booksellers Directory*
Sheppard Press (ed). *Dealers in Books* (Annual)
Sheppard, J. and J. *International Directory of Book Collectors, 1980* (Sheppard Press)
Ward, A. and P. *The Small Publisher* (Oleander, 1979)
PERIODICAL: *The Bookseller* (weekly, J. Whitaker & Sons, Ltd)

Terms and Terminology

Glaister, G. A. *Glaister's Glossary of the Book* (Allen & Unwin, 1979)
Jacob, H. A. *A Pocket Dictionary of Publishing Terms* (Macdonald and Jane's, 1976)

Independent and Little Presses

Small Press Record of Books in Print (Dustbooks, 1982)
Smith, E. Lucie. *The Little Press Movement in England and America* (Turret Books, 1972)
PERIODICALS: PALPI (Poetry and Little Press Information — Association of Little Presses: twice a year approximately)
Small Press Magazine (quarterly, R. R. Bowker Co, 205E 42nd Street, New York, NY 10017, USA)

Private Presses

Bellamy, B. *Private Presses and Publishing in England since 1945* (Clive Bingley Co)
Cave, R. *The Private Press* (Faber, 1971)
Cunard, Nancy. *These Were the Hours, memoirs of my Press* (Univ of Illinois, 1964)

185

Nin, Anaïs. *The Story of my Printing Press* (from *In Praise of the Sensitive Man*) (W. H. Allen, 1980)

Westreich, B. *Directory of Private Presses* (Arden Park Press, 1983)

Woolf, L. 'An Autobiography' (from *The Hogarth Press,* pp 169–260) (Penguin, 1980)

PERIODICALS: *Albion* (Ed: R. Burford Mason, 26 West Hill, Hitchin; three times a year)

Private Press Books (a record and illustrations of new books from private presses; annual: Private Libraries Association)

Small-Magazine Production

Beach, M. *Editing your Newsletter* (Dustbooks, 1982)

Fulton, L. and Ferber, E. (ed). *International Directory of Small Magazines* (Dustbooks, 1982)

Into Print, a guide to Non-Commercial Newspapers and Magazines (Teach Yourself Books Ltd, 1968)

Wyckoff, E. H. *Editing and Producing the Small Publication* (Van Nostrand, 1956)

Editing

Avis, F. C. *Bookman's Concise Dictionary* (Avis, 1956)

Butcher, J. *Copy-Editing* (CUP, 1978)

Collins Gem Dictionary of Spelling and Word Division (Collins, 1968)

Hart's Rules for Compositors and Readers (OUP, 1974)

Oxford Dictionary for Writers and Editors (OUP, 1981)

Authorship and Publishing

Directory of Grantmaking Trusts (Charities Aid Foundation)

Flint, M. F. *Users' Guide to Copyright* (Butterworths, 1979)

Smith, Keith. *Marketing for Small Publishers* (Inter-Action, 1983)

Tarr, J. C. *How to Plan Print* (Crosby, Lockwood, 1938)

Thomas, D. St J. *Non-Fiction: A Guide to Writing and Publishing* (David & Charles/Harper, 1974)

Thorp, J. *Printing for Business* (Hogg & Co, 1919)

Designing

Lewis, J. *Graphic Design* (Routledge, 1954)

McLean, R. *Typography* (Thames and Hudson, 1980)

Moran, J. *The Composition of Reading Matter* (Wace, 1965)

Shepherd. E. G. *Design and Print* (Macdonald and Evans, 1963)

Simon, O. *Introduction to Typography* (Faber, 1963)

Williamson, H. *The Design of Books* (OUP, 1963)

—— *Methods of Book Design*, 3rd ed (Yale Univ Press), 1983)

PERIODICAL: *Penrose Annual* Review of the Graphic Arts (Lund Humphries: annual)

Offset-Lithography

Paste-up and Artwork

Burke, C. *Printing It* (Ballantine Books, 1972)

Cohen, C. *Print It!* (Kaye-Ward, 1982)

Graham, W. B. *Complete Guide to Paste-Up* (Canimpex, 1983)

Van Uchelin, R. *Paste-Up* (Van Nostrand, 1976)

Zeitlin, J. *Print, how you can do it yourself* (Inter-Action, 1980)

Process Camera Work

Burden, J. *Graphic Reproduction Photography* (Focal Press, 1973)

Chambers, E. *Camera and Process Work* (Benn, 1964)

Kodak Graphic Arts Handbook (Kodak Ltd, 1973)

Lithography and Small Offset

Goodacre, D. *Small Offset* (Wyven Press, 1969)

Faux, I. *Modern Lithography* (Macdonald & Evans, 1973)

Pilborough, D. *Small Offset for Beginners* (Canimpex, 1982)

PERIODICAL: *The Small Printer* (British Printing Society, BM/ISPA, London WC1: monthly)

Letterpress Printing

Adana Ltd. *Type and Typesetting for users of Adana Printing Machines* (Twickenham, 1980)

Atkins, W. (ed). *Art & Practice of Printing,* Vols 1, 2, 4 and 6 (New Era Co)

Basic Printing (Letterpress) (British Printing Society, 1980)

Gillham, A. *Craft for Schools* (instructions for building a press) (Pitman, 1933)

Goodyear, F. *Printing and Bookcrafts for Schools* (build your own press) (Harrap, 1930)

Instruction Manual: Reproduction & Nyloprint (BASF Ltd, 1978)

Liebermann, J. B. *Printing as a Hobby* (Oak Tree Press, 1963)

Pickering, C. L. *Printing, theory and practice,* Vols 2 and 4 (Pitman, 1958)

Ryder, J. *Printing for Pleasure* (Bodley Head, 1976)

Simon, H. and Carter, H. *Printing Explained* (a handbook for schools and amateurs) (Dryad, 1931)

Simon, H. *Introduction to Printing* (Faber, 1968)

Southward, J. *Modern Printing,* Vol 1 (R. Lawrence, 1926)

NB   Manuals on letterpress printing are now mostly out of print. Suppliers of secondhand books on printing generally, are: Tony Appleton Ltd of Brighton, and Keith Hogg of Tenterden, Kent.

Calligraphy

Biggs, J. R. *Lettercraft* (Blandford, 1982)

Johnson, E. *Writing and Illuminated Lettering* (Pitman, 1906)

West, A. *Written by Hand* (Allen and Unwin, 1951)

Illustration

Biggs, J. R. *The Craft of Woodcuts* (Blandford, 1963)

Chamberlain, W. *Etching and Engraving* (Thames and Hudson, 1972)
Dobson, M. *Blockmaking and Printing by Hand* (Pitman, 1945)
Dover Books: *Dover Pictorial Archives Series* (Dover/Constable, 1980)
    Pictorial Calligraphy and ornamentation
Hinwood, T. *Advertising art* (David & Charles, 1973)
Hutton, W. *Making Woodcuts* (Academy Editions, 1974)
Kent, C. *Starting with Relief Printmaking* (Studio Vista, 1970)
Kinsey, A. *Introducing screen printing* (Batsford, 1967)
Lamb, L. *Drawing for Illustration* (OUP, 1962)
Lewis, J. *A Handbook of Type and Illustration* (Faber, 1956)
Mills, V. *Making Posters* (Studio Vista, 1967)
O'Connor, J. *Introducing Relief Printing* (Batsford, 1973)
Severin, M. *Your wood engraving* (Sylvan Press, 1953)
Van Heuar, A. *Relief Printing* (Museum Press, 1960)

Home Papermaking

Kern, M. *The Complete Book of Hand-crafted paper* (Coward McCann, 1980)
Turner, S. and Skiold, B. *Handmade Paper Today* (Lund Humphries, 1983)

Bookbinding

Burdett, E. *The Craft of Bookbinding* (David & Charles, 1975)
Colins, A. *Book Crafts for Schools* (Dryad, 1959)

Reference Libraries

Mark Longman Library, National Book League, Book House, 45 East Hill, London SW18
St Bride's Printing Library, Brides Lane, London EC4

NOTE TO AMERICAN READERS

Our happy visits to American friends and colleagues suggest that the problems, joys and sorrows of publishing for fun as well as for profit are similar to those experienced in Britain. However, the small-press, private-press and little-press scene in North America is proportionately larger than in Britain, and is growing both in range and sophistication. We hope, therefore, that a book such as ours may be of interest to some American readers and beginners.

Clearly, however, where we quote the prices of second-hand equipment and of services, we cannot provide American equivalents in dollars since the entire market situation is different, not only as between America and Britain, but to a degree within the American continent itself. Further, in the United States there are many more established suppliers specialising in catering to the amateur and small-printer market. We hope the time-and-cost economics will even so prove broadly helpful.

We have rather insularly adhered to British spellings of common printing terms to save complicating our pages. Most American typophiles know that their fonts are our founts and their typos are our errors, too! There is a fair interchange between small presses across the Atlantic, as there is between the professionals; long may it continue.

ACKNOWLEDGEMENTS

It would be impossible to list all the publishers, booksellers and printers — in Britain and abroad — who have helped us with this book, for our ideas have been shaped by visits and conversations about this subject over many years.

We would like, however, to mention the helpful and friendly advice given by the professional printers and staffs of Berkshire College of Art, Reading, and Twickenham College of Technology (now Richmond-upon-Thames College) Printing Departments, and we also wish to thank the following friends who have contributed ideas and pictures or have vetted chapters in draft: Julius Stafford-Baker, David Chambers, Bob Cobbing, Simon Colverson, John Cotton, Morris Cox, Don Goodacre, Gestetner Ltd, Stanislaw Gliwa, Denis McLeavy, Charles Maude, Walter Partridge, John Randle, Roneo Alcatel Ltd, Peter and Carola Scupham, Toni Savage, Bernard Stone, Graham Sykes, Alan Tarling, Michael Taylor, David Tipton, Alan and Joan Tucker, Tony Ward, Ivor Waters, Paul Witherington, G. Barrasford Young.

R. L., J. B. E.

INDEX

Page numbers in *italic* refer to illustrations